PHYSICS
PROJECTS FOR YOUNG SCIENTISTS

PETER H. GOODWIN

PHYSICS PROJECTS FOR YOUNG SCIENTISTS

FRANKLIN WATTS
NEW YORK / LONDON / TORONTO / SYDNEY / 1991

Library of Congress Cataloging-in-Publication Data

Goodwin, Peter,
Physics projects for young scientists / Peter H. Goodwin.
p. cm.—(Projects for young scientists)
Includes bibliographical references and index.
Summary: Gives instructions for and explains the principles behind
a variety of simple physics experiments.
ISBN 0-531-11070-2
1. Physics—Experiments—Juvenile literature.   2. Physics—
Experiments—Methodology—Juvenile literature.   [1. Physics—
Experiments.   2. Experiments.]   I. Title.   II. Series.
QC25.G66   1991
530'.078—dc20
91-17822
CIP
AC

CONTENTS

PHYSICS
PROJECTS FOR YOUNG SCIENTISTS

1

PHYSICS AND EXPERIMENTS

Physics is the study of how matter and energy interact. Because everything in the universe is either matter or energy, this could mean that physics is the study of everything. Actually, physicists don't study everything; what they do study is how objects behave under varying conditions. A physicist analyzes forces, motion, and energy exchanges of objects of various sizes. The objects range in size from much smaller than atoms to as large as the universe.

The word "physics" scares many people even though everyone has studied it since they were babies. A baby performs simple experiments as it rattles a rattle: it adds energy to some matter and thereby produces noise, a form of energy. Later, the child performs more complex experiments as it builds blocks into towers and then knocks them down.

We use physics principles daily, so studying physics is quite natural. We learn indirectly about center of gravity, a physics principle, because in order to walk we need the center of gravity to be over our feet. We fall down if it's not. Many people don't know the term "center of gravity" but they work with it every day. To do simple experiments you don't need to know all the terms physicists use. However, as your observations and experiments become more involved, more-precise words may help to more clearly describe the things you see. Knowing more about physics also allows you to investigate things more quickly and perhaps reach better conclusions.

Some experiments require you to use numbers, although often the math is quite easy. One thing you should remember is that math is only a tool scientists use. It is not needed for all experiments, and you can draw good conclusions from experiments even though you are not a math whiz. Only a few of the projects in this book require more than basic math.

As you work on these experiments, keep in mind that sometimes it's hard to get answers immediately. It takes time to work out solutions to some problems. If an experiment doesn't work, try to think about why things are happening the way they do. Sometimes a single, careless mistake can cause large problems. Have patience and think about what you are doing.

You may need a bit of courage to run these experiments because sometimes an experiment will fail. When the experiment doesn't work, something happened which you didn't understand or do correctly. However, the failures are sometimes important and often lead to discoveries which are unexpected. Remember, science doesn't always move along smoothly.

This book helps you to approach your investigations in the proper way. It helps you ask questions and get started on a basic experiment, which can then lead to other experiments. After you have done the basic experiments, the book will help you to draw conclusions from your data. Finally, it suggests further investigations.

Chapters contain related projects with background material to help you understand the experiments. Each project has a basic experiment or two and then suggestions for further projects. At the end of each chapter containing projects, suggestions are given for other experiments related to the topic. You can do these experiments using what you have learned from running the other experiments.

Each project is meant as a starting point and should lead you to new questions. Some of the basic experiments can be done quickly and are suitable for a classroom science project. Others may take more time, so you may have to work on them during weekends or vacations. Some extensions of the projects can be used for science fair projects although the basic investigations probably are not original enough for you to be the winner in a large science fair.

You can do these projects for any reason you choose. The only requirement is an interest in the world around you. You may want to do only the experiments outlined here, or you may decide to work on more-complicated experiments. You may find that your own ideas work better than the descriptions given here.

Now that you have an idea about what you are going to find in this book, it's time to start running experiments. Don't forget to enjoy your investigations. Some people enjoy doing investigations so much that they spend their lives running experiments. We call these people scientists. Others run experiments of their own just for fun. We call them scientists, too.

2

WORKING SCIENTIFICALLY

Scientists work in different ways, but the process which goes on in their minds is similar. They ask questions, gather data, and then try to answer their questions. This is similar to how most people solve problems, but scientists usually follow a more formal procedure.

If you say "Can I buy a bicycle?" you are forming a hypothesis. You then collect data to see if it's possible for you to buy one. You think about how much money you can spend and check the prices of the bicycles which interest you. Collecting the data may be easy or hard. The more data you collect, the more sure about your conclusion you will be. Your conclusion, or the answer to your question, is that you are or are not able to buy the bicycle.

The example of buying a bicycle is a simple form of what scientists do. They study something and develop questions they want to investigate. "Gee, I wonder if this ball will bounce higher on a cement floor or a lawn?" A hypothesis would be: "I think the ball will bounce higher on concrete." This is a guess at an answer which you then test with an experiment. You would collect data by dropping the ball on cement and measuring the height it bounced, and then repeating the procedure on a lawn. After taking the data, you make a conclusion based on the data.

Scientists have to be careful to make sure that their data is valid. Scientists use "controls" for this purpose. The control allows you to compare one result with another. If you dropped the ball onto concrete from a height of 0.5 m (1.6 ft) but dropped the ball onto the lawn from 2m (6.6 ft), the ball might bounce higher on the lawn but you wouldn't be proving anything. To run a "controlled" experiment, change only one thing, or variable, at a time. If you change the surface onto which you drop the ball, don't change the height from which you drop it too.

Using a control is very important in scientific work. Many improper conclusions have been drawn because there was no "control" for comparison. As you run your experiments, think about what you change in an experiment. If you use a different ball, you may be changing the mass and size, either of which may change the way it bounces. Your data may support your conclusions but for the wrong reasons.

As you run experiments, you should follow the scientific method. Develop a hypothesis, plan your experiment carefully, and run it to collect data. Make careful measurements and record the data in a notebook. Using a notebook is better than pieces of paper because you may lose pieces of paper and a book will keep the data together. If the data collected by running a careful experiment supports your hypothesis, then your hypothesis may be true. On the other hand, your data may show that your hypothesis was incorrect.

You should remember that you may never be able to *prove* your hypothesis. Some questions may remain unsolved or untested. Even the great physicist Albert Einstein made mistakes as he worked, and sometimes his theories did not completely explain the world and the universe. There are always some unanswered questions that others will have to answer.

FOR FURTHER READING

Gardner, Robert. *Ideas for Science Projects*. New York: Franklin Watts, 1986.

Gardner, Robert. *More Ideas for Science Projects*. New York: Franklin Watts, 1989.

Herbert, Don. *Mr. Wizard's Experiments for Young Scientists*. New York: Doubleday, 1959.

Hewitt, Paul. *Conceptual Physics*. New York: Little, Brown, 1981.

Strong, Clair. *The Scientific American Book of Projects for the Amateur Scientist*. New York: Simon and Schuster, 1960.

UNESCO. *700 Science Experiments for Everyone*. Compiled by UNESCO. New York: Doubleday, 1958.

3

THE STUDY OF MECHANICS

The study of forces and motion is called mechanics. Sir Isaac Newton (1642–1727), whom some call the founder of the study of mechanics, was the first person to mathematically relate forces exerted on objects to their motion. His famous equation $f = ma$ shows that the force (f) exerted on an object of mass (m) is related to its acceleration (a). A force is a push or a pull; all objects have mass which resists a change in motion; and acceleration shows how an object's motion changes with time.

In order to start a car moving from a stop sign, you push on the accelerator pedal. The engine causes a force, and the car (which has mass) starts to move. Because it was stationary and then starts to move, it accelerates or changes its motion. Pushing more on the accelerator pedal makes the engine exert more force, causing faster acceleration. Other objects have their motion changed by forces, too. A ball hit by a bat has its motion changed by the force from the bat. Because the ball exerts a force on the bat, the bat also changes its motion.

Investigations in mechanics will help you to understand the laws of physics better. You may discover things you didn't know before or see them more clearly. The projects which follow are only a few of the possible experiments. They can be expanded as you find out something which makes you ask another question. You may be able to modify the apparatus to answer your questions, or sometimes you may have to design completely new apparatus.

Remember to have fun but make sure to make careful observations and measurements. Record your data so you can look back on it at a later time. If you are careless you may draw improper conclusions, which will make it harder to continue with your investigations. A little extra time spent in running your experiments and making careful measurements may help in the long run.

WHAT AFFECTS FRICTION?
IS A SMOOTH SURFACE ALWAYS BETTER?

Friction is a part of our lives. We need it to do many things, but often we try to reduce it. Cars need friction to start, stop, and go around corners, but too much friction in the engine or other moving parts makes the car stop running very quickly.

Sometimes, something increases friction in some circumstances and decreases it in others. Throwing sand on ice increases friction between the tires and the ice. However, throwing sand on dry pavement decreases friction between the tires and the road. You may have noticed this as you skidded going around a sandy corner on a bicycle. Why do these differences occur?

In a similar way, making surfaces smoother tends to cause less friction, but only up to a point. To make a sled's runners slide more easily, you make them smoother. However, if you make two metal surfaces very, very smooth and place them in contact with one another, it is hard to slide one across the other.

Two basic things cause friction: interlocking parts of the objects (like two pieces of sandpaper), and electrical forces between the atoms of the objects (which occurs only when the atoms are very close to each other). Running some experiments may help you to find out more about it. Try to develop a hypothesis about what factors affect friction and in what way. Then, experiment to see if your predictions were correct. Start by running the simple experiments outlined below and then, if you are interested in testing more theories, try some of the other projects or ones you design on your own.

MATERIALS AND TOOLS
1-inch × 6-inch/(2.5 cm × 15 cm) board about 1½ feet (45 cm) long (it must have a uniform surface)
table or other flat surface
block of wood 2 or 3 inches (5–7.5 cm) on a side
plastic protractor
various other objects which can be placed on the board
various things to change the surface of the ramp

PROCEDURE
   Note: When recording data for these experiments, include the angle, the object, and the surface used for sliding.
   Make a ramp with the board as shown in Figure 1. Place the block of wood on the board and then slowly raise the board until the block starts slipping down the ramp. With the protractor, measure the angle the board makes with the table. Record the appropriate data.
   Repeat the experiment a couple of times, placing the block on the same side each time to find the average angle at which the block slides.
   What will happen if you slide the block on a side with a different surface area? Test this to see if your hypothesis is correct. Repeat the experiment to check your results. Record your data. Was your hypothesis correct?

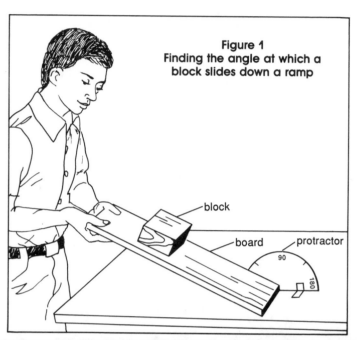

Figure 1
Finding the angle at which a
block slides down a ramp

block

board

protractor

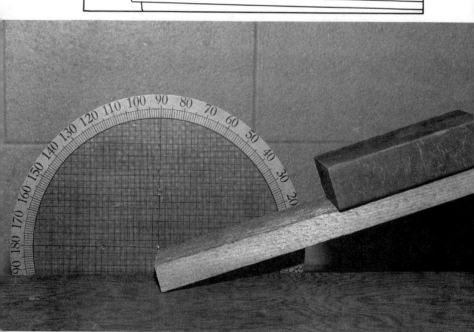

Try different objects and measure the angle at which they slide down the ramp. Try to predict the angle before you experiment. Include an ice cube in your experiments. As you experiment with different objects, see if you can put them into categories. This may help you make better predictions.

Now change the surface of the ramp. You might sprinkle sand on the ramp, tape some writing paper or sandpaper on the board, or put a liquid such as water on it. **(Use only safe liquids such as water, salad oil, or milk. Check with an adult to make sure that your materials are safe and won't stain and make sure you clean up afterward.)** As you do your experiments, try to predict which surfaces and which objects will require the largest or smallest angle to slide.

Physicists describe how large friction is with the "coefficient of friction," the ratio of the force of friction to the force between the surfaces. The larger the coefficient of friction, the larger the force required to push or pull an object along a surface or, in the case of this experiment, the steeper the ramp must be before the object slides.

When an object slides down a ramp, the coefficient of friction equals the tangent of the angle at which an object just begins to slide. Tangents can be found using most calculators. Find the coefficients of friction for your experiments and record the values on your data table.

After you have worked with a number of different surfaces and objects, try to find objects which will have the largest and the smallest coefficients of friction. Realize that if you raise the ramp to a 90-degree angle and the object doesn't slide, that friction is not what is keeping it there.

A block moving down a ramp can be a simple experiment on the effects of friction.

Try finding the tangent of 90 degrees on your calculator. Try finding the tangent of 89.9999 degrees. What is your result?

OTHER PROJECTS WITH FRICTION

1. Experiment with different shoe treads on different surfaces. Are some shoes better than others? Is one kind of tread good for all situations?

2. Examine how different size grains of sand affect how things slide down ramps made of ice, and see how the temperature of the ice changes the results.

3. Examine how road salt affects the coefficient of friction and why road crews must watch the air temperature to see if they should spread salt. Experiment at different temperatures. Obviously, this is easier to do if you live where the temperatures go below freezing.

4. Examine how different tire treads behave on different surfaces, and see if you can predict which treads are better. Can you make a better tire tread?

5. Pull different things through the water and investigate how the frictional force changes with different shapes and speeds.

6. Slide a rough block of wood down a wooden ramp and measure the coefficient of friction. Then repeat the same action a number of times after sanding down the sliding surface of the block a little each time. The idea is to see how the coefficient of friction changes as the block becomes smoother. Run the experiment until the block surface is very smooth. (You can also do a similar experiment by gradually sanding the surface of the ramp instead of the block.)

MEASURING ACCELERATIONS
IN THE REAL WORLD

We often experience acceleration. Sometimes it is uncomfortable, while at other times we pay money to be accelerated in strange ways. Large accelerations, such as those in a car crash, can cause pain and injury. But in other situations, amusement park rides, for example, such accelerations can be exciting and enjoyable.

Under what conditions are accelerations enjoyable or painful? What is the smallest acceleration you can feel? What is the largest you normally experience driving a car? What makes an acceleration in an amusement park ride exciting?

Acceleration can often be measured approximately by a simple apparatus you can make yourself. Using this device, called an accelerometer, you can investigate how you feel when various accelerations occur. You can then analyze accelerations which give particular sensations to try to reach some generalizations about driving, riding bicycles, amusement park rides, etc.

Start with simple questions and then, once you are familiar with the apparatus, you can go on to bigger and better experiments. If you plan to go to an amusement park, make sure to experiment with your apparatus before you leave home so that you can fix any problems beforehand.

MATERIALS AND TOOLS
plastic protractor
piece of cardboard
pen
scissors
glue or tape
string
weight
spring (should stretch 1 or 2 cm if a large washer is on it)
metal washer 2–3 cm (about 1 in) in diameter
meterstick

PROCEDURE
Place the protractor on the cardboard and trace its shape with the pen. Then put the angles (0°, 10°, 20°, etc.)

at the appropriate places on your cardboard just outside of the protractor's edge. Remove the protractor from the cardboard and then, as shown in Figure 2, carefully put the numbers inside the tracing of the protractor to form an acceleration scale. Cut out the cardboard and tape it to the protractor.

Now, tie the string through the hole as shown in the diagram and hang a weight from the other end of the string. It should be free to swing and be about 1 or 2 cm longer than the radius of the protractor.

Make another accelerometer by taping your spring to a piece of cardboard. Mark the cardboard at the bottom of the spring −10 with the pencil. Now, attach the washer to the end of the spring with tape and mark its position against the cardboard as 0. Measure the distance between the −10 mark and the 0 mark. As shown

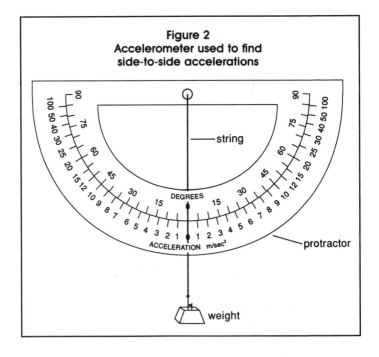

Figure 2
Accelerometer used to find
side-to-side accelerations

in Figure 3, add the numbers +10, +20, etc., to the cardboard so that the same distance separates each number from the next one as separates −10 from 0.

The accelerometers measure in the units of m/sec^2. An acceleration of 10 m/sec^2 means that you *change* your velocity by 10 meters per second every second. Changing your velocity 10 m per second for .1 second would change your velocity 1 m per second. When you jump into the air, gravity pulls you back to Earth with an acceleration of 10 m/sec^2. Initially, you are moving upward and then you are moving downward so your velocity changes from up to

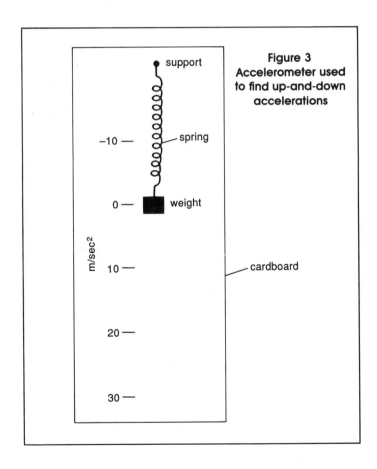

**Figure 3
Accelerometer used
to find up-and-down
accelerations**

support

spring

−10 —

0 — weight

m/sec^2

10 — cardboard

20 —

30 —

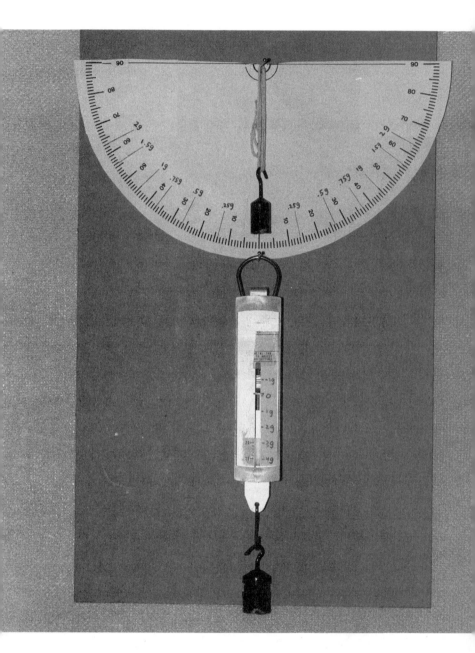

Make your own personal accelerometer (see Figure 2).

down. You must have accelerated. If your velocity is constant, then your acceleration is zero. This means your acceleration is zero if you are stationary or if you are moving at a constant velocity in one direction. If the velocity remains the same, the acceleration must be zero.

Run some experiments with your accelerometers. First use the one made with the protractor by holding the flat edge level. It must be held level whenever you make a reading. When you are stationary, it should read zero. Now, walk at a *constant* velocity in a straight line. What does it read? Record what it reads and what you are doing on a data table.

Now, hold your accelerometer so the flat edge points in the direction you will walk. Starting from rest, move so the accelerometer reads 1 m/sec^2. What do you feel with the acceleration? What happens before too long? Record your observations and include the fact that you were giving yourself 1 m/sec^2 acceleration.

Accelerations that occur when you move in a circle are called centripetal accelerations because they are toward the center of a circle. Velocity has direction so when you change your direction, you change your velocity. This change in velocity results in an acceleration.

To experience centripetal acceleration, mark a circle 1 m in radius on the floor or ground. Hold your protractor so the flat edge points toward the center of the circle and walk at a speed which causes a 1 m/sec^2 acceleration. Record your observations and feelings. Repeat the experiment for other centripetal accelerations.

The accelerations you have experienced so far are in the horizontal plane. Now, use the spring accelerometer to investigate accelerations in the vertical direction. Hold the accelerometer near the floor and then raise it with a constant 1 m/sec^2 acceleration. Use the average position for your measurement. Try to move smoothly to get a constant reading, although it may be hard to do. Record your observations. Repeat this with different accelerations.

OTHER PROJECTS WITH ACCELEROMETERS

1. Take your accelerometers in a car and see what accelerations occur as the car starts and stops, turns and goes over bumps. Make note of the sensations and measurements associated with these accelerations.

2. Use your accelerometers to find the accelerations you can experience on a bicycle. What are the maximum values for acceleration you find? Under what conditions do you feel no acceleration?

3. Take your accelerometers to an amusement park and measure the accelerations you experience on a roller coaster. **Make sure to be careful as you take your data. Don't risk being injured for the cause of science.** You may have to ride the roller coaster a couple of times to get good readings. Record the values for various parts of the ride along with the sensations you feel. If the amusement park has a second roller coaster, ride it too. Before you ride, see if you can predict the values for acceleration you will experience. Again, note the sensations you feel during the ride.

4. Try other amusement park rides to measure their accelerations. Remember, if the accelerations are abrupt, such as a collision in bumper cars, the accelerometers will read twice the actual acceleration. **Make sure that you are careful and don't risk injury as you take your data.**

5. Build an accelerometer which uses a spring but leaves a mark at the maximum displacement. This will allow you to find values for acceleration in collisions which you can't or shouldn't experience. You may be able to devise a device to measure the acceleration that results as a ball hits a bat.

COLLISIONS:
WHAT HAPPENS AFTERWARD

Collisions occur every day. Some are considered good, and some are bad. A good collision occurs when you hit a home run with a baseball bat. Car collisions in which people are hurt and cars destroyed are obviously bad.

Many sports involve collisions of one form or another, and we often experience them as we move about in our daily activities. But what makes for good ones or bad ones? And how can good collisions be improved and bad ones made less harmful? Why can you hit a baseball farther if you use a metal bat instead of a wooden one? Car manufacturers try to make cars safer in crashes, but how do they run their investigations?

Answering some of these questions in general terms is quite easy, but dealing with specific facts is much harder. For example, how much more damage occurs if a car is going 1 mile (1.6 km) per hour faster when it collides with a tree? Any differences may be hard to find because differences may be slight. Also, the investigator may need to actually crash a few cars to get the answers, which would be quite expensive and potentially dangerous!

Try to develop a hypothesis as to what happens after two things collide and then see if your hypothesis is correct. What conditions allow you to hit a home run? How could you design the bat and ball to make it easier or harder to hit a home run? Run the simple experiments and then try working on these questions. So, get started with the experiment and then you will get ideas for other questions. The conclusions you draw from the simple experiments may lead you to other experiments.

MATERIALS AND TOOLS
baseball bat
rope or string
support stand made of wood (if you don't build this yourself, find an old table you have permission to use)
balls of various kinds
plastic protractor
meterstick
tape
weights

PROCEDURE

Tie a string to the handle end of the baseball bat so you can hang the bat from a support. If you experiment outside, you can hang it from a tree; otherwise, you can hang it from a nail driven into the wood molding of a doorway, but **ask permission to drive the nail.**

Arrange the support stand to hold the various balls you have collected. Place a ball at the stand's edge. Hang the bat so it will hit the ball and not the stand. The ball should move horizontally after it is hit, as shown in Figure 4.

Now, pull the bat so the string makes an angle of 30 degrees. Release the bat so it swings smoothly and makes contact with the ball. Measure the distance to where the ball landed from a point directly under the ball's initial po-

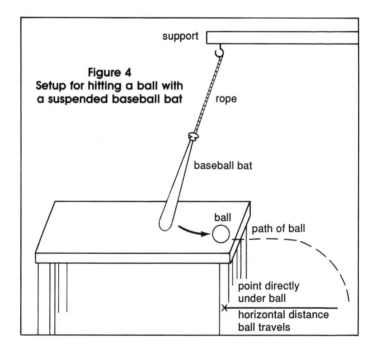

support

**Figure 4
Setup for hitting a ball with
a suspended baseball bat**

rope

baseball bat

ball

path of ball

point directly
under ball

horizontal distance
ball travels

sition. Repeat the experiment a couple of times, making the ball move in approximately the same direction after the collision. (You may have to practice a bit to have this happen.) Find the average distance the ball flew. Record each distance and the average value.

What happens if the bat is moving faster? Try pulling the bat back to different angles and find the average distance the ball travels before hitting the ground. Record the distances and the angle from which the bat swung. Did the ball behave as you expected? Try to predict how far the ball will go when the bat is pulled to a different angle. Check your prediction.

Now, use a different ball and predict how it will behave. How will its mass and the material it is made from affect the results? Test your hypothesis and record the results. Include the ball's mass and a description of it.

You have been looking only at how the ball behaves after the collision. Repeat your experiments but measure how the bat moves. Sometimes it may move backward after the collision rather than forward. Can you predict before you run the experiment in what direction the bat will move? What factors affect how the bat moves after the collision?

You can quantify your results more by finding the actual velocities of the bat and ball. The velocity of the ball is related to the distance it travels before it hits the floor. If it travels twice as far, it is going twice as fast. The actual velocity is found by dividing the distance it moves by the time it takes to fall to the floor (assuming it starts moving horizontally). The time is found by using the equation $t = \sqrt{4.9h}$ where t is the time in seconds and h is the height in meters from which the ball falls.

The velocity of the bat can be approximated by the equation $v = \sqrt{9.8h}$ where v is in m/sec and h is the difference in height in meters between where the lower end of the bat is released and its lowest point.

Change the mass of the bat by taping weights to it. Make a hypothesis about how this will change the collision, and then test it.

OTHER PROJECTS
WITH COLLISIONS

1. Use a bat made from a different material and see what differences occur in the collision between the bat and the ball. Make a bat which will hit a ball farthest with a given amount of swing. Would your bat be good in a game?

2. Devise a way to make the batted ball move only a small amount. What materials should you use and how should you construct the ball? Would these materials be good for protecting people in auto accidents?

3. Relate your experiments to kicking a soccer ball. What part of the foot should hit it? What should the foot be doing as it hits the ball? Do good soccer players do this?

4. If energy is conserved, a collision is an "elastic" collision. If it is lost, it is called "inelastic." Lost energy generally does work on the objects which collide. If you are in an inelastic collision, work is done on your body which may break a bone or at least cause pain. See if kinetic energy is lost in a particular collision by finding the initial kinetic energy and comparing it to the final kinetic energy of the *two* objects after collision (add the energy from each object). The kinetic energy, or energy of motion, is found using the equation $K.E. = \frac{1}{2}mv^2$, where m is mass in kilograms and v is velocity in m/sec. Which collisions lose the most energy? The least?

5. Design apparatus so both objects move before the collision. You might want to have both objects on ropes and have them swing toward each other. What happens to the energy in these collisions? Try modeling the collision of a boxing glove with a boxer's body. See what happens

when the boxer is moving both toward the glove and away from it.

6. When a pool ball is hit by a cue ball, the cue ball may be rolling. How is this different from a collision with a nonrolling ball? Design an experiment to model this kind of collision.

7. When a car collides with a brick wall, the front end of the car collapses and acts as a mass between the people in the car and the brick wall. Experiment to see how each object in a chain reaction moves after its collision. Energy must be transferred to the second object and then to the third. Does the result of your experiment show why rear-engine cars (with little mass in front of the driver) are not produced now.

HOW THINGS BOUNCE:
THE COEFFICIENT OF RESTITUTION

Many games involve balls which bounce off either a bat, the floor, the ground, rackets, or each other. The way a ball bounces determines how the game is played. Playing tennis with "dead" tennis balls, which bounce very little, makes the game different, and, most people think, less enjoyable. On the other hand, if a baseball bounced as high as a live tennis ball when dropped onto a hard surface, every baseball park in the work would have to be made larger!

How can you describe the way a ball bounces? The technical term for it is the "coefficient of restitution." This describes how the speed of the ball changes after a collision. If a ball hits the ground moving at 10 m/sec and leaves it going at 7 m/sec, its coefficient of restitution is .7 $(7/10 = .7)$. This is the typical coefficient of restitution of a new tennis ball. A "superball" has a coefficient of restitution nearly equal to 1. It's so "super" because it leaves a hard surface going at nearly the same speed as when it

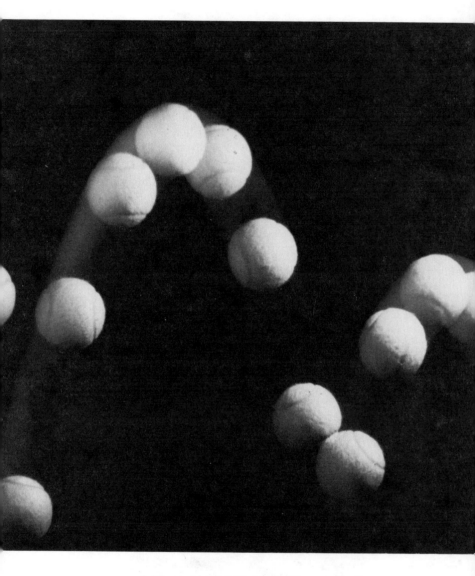

A bouncing tennis ball with parabolic
trajectory and constant acceleration.
This is a time-lapse photo taken with
stroboscopic lighting.

hits the ground. If it's dropped on a hard surface, it keeps bouncing for a long time. At the other extreme is a squash ball, which hardly bounces at all. Using a superball in a squash court would be dangerous because the ball would zip around and it would be hard to avoid being hit.

But what kind of balls bounce best? What difference does the surface they bounce on make? Develop a hypothesis as to how balls bounce and then test your hypothesis by running an experiment such as the one outlined below. Make careful measurements and record them in a notebook. Start by asking simple questions and then experiment to test your hypothesis. First, you will investigate the different values for coefficients of restitution, and then you will investigate what causes the differences you find.

MATERIALS AND TOOLS
two tennis balls, one new and one dead
any three kinds of balls, such as a golf ball, rubber ball, and foam-rubber ball
meterstick
hard surfaces on which to drop the balls
piece of paper
heavy weight

PROCEDURES
Take any of the three miscellaneous balls and drop it from a height of 1 m (3 ft). Measure the height to which the ball bounces off a hard surface. Record this value, identifying the ball you are using. Then, drop the ball a few more times to see if your results are consistent.

Repeat the experiment with the other two balls in turn.

Now, find the average height to which each ball rose. This average height is used to find the coefficient of restitution (CR) using the following equation: $CR = \sqrt{h}$. (This equation works because the initial height is 1 m. If you were using a different initial height, you would have to use the equation $CR = \sqrt{(h_{up}/h_{down})}$, where h_{up} is the height the ball bounces up and h_{down} is the distance it falls.)

Different balls should have different coefficients of restitution because the balls were made in different ways or have changed their nature since they were made. How do the coefficients of restitution differ between the balls? What might cause the differences?

Put those balls aside for the moment and take the tennis balls. Place the new one on a piece of paper and trace the shape of the part touching the paper. Then place a heavy weight like a large stone, a log, or a bucket of water on top of the ball. Trace the shape of the part of the ball touching the paper now. Remove the weight and the tennis ball and label this tracing as the "new ball." Repeat the procedure for the dead tennis ball.

What differences do you notice in the tracings? Do the tracings help explain how the balls bounce? When a ball bounces, molecules in the ball rub past each other and energy is lost. The more they rub, the more energy they lose. Does this explain why the balls bounce different amounts? Try tracing the shape of the other three balls with no weight on them and then with weight on them. What do you find?

Now, examine how different surfaces allow various balls to bounce. Drop the new tennis ball on a variety of surfaces, such as a concrete floor, a wood floor, carpets, etc. Find the ball's coefficient of restitution for these surfaces. Does this mean that playing tennis might be different on different surfaces? How does the coefficient of restitution change for the other balls when the surface is changed?

OTHER PROJECTS
WITH BOUNCING BALLS

1. Some kinds of balls can be pumped up to change the air pressure inside them. Examples include basketballs, soccer balls, volleyballs, and some brands of tennis balls.

Develop a hypothesis for how the air pressure will affect the coefficient of restitution. **(Be careful not to put too much air pressure in the ball or it may burst.)**

2. Suppose you wanted to design a new form of tennis to be played on a court half as big as the regular court. Taking into account that players must be able to hit the ball with a racket on this smaller court, figure out what coefficient of restitution you would like to have. Test your hypothesis with some friends.

3. A dropped ball normally bounces a number of times before it comes to rest. Find how the coefficient of restitution is related to the total number of bounces a ball takes. It may be hard counting the last, small bounces so you can set some limit on the size of the bounce. For example, if you drop the ball from 1 m, you might count the bounces until they are only .01 m high.

4. Try playing a game you know how to play with a ball with a different coefficient of restitution, say half as large or twice as large. Try to describe how the game becomes different and how it stays the same.

5. Examine how a new tennis ball bounces off a tennis racket in different situations. Try resting the racket tip on the floor while holding the handle firmly in your hand. When you bounce the ball off the racket, what differences do you expect and what differences occur? What happens if the racket is moving toward the ball?

HOW ROTATIONAL MOTION IS CHANGED: GOOD AND BAD TORQUES

Some things are meant to turn while others aren't. When you push on bicycle pedals, you expect the wheels to turn. You also want a screw to turn as it goes into a piece of wood but then to stay in place. When you hit a tennis shot, however, you don't want your racket to turn because you may hit the ball in the wrong direction. Tennis rackets can be designed to keep them from turning on impact.

Even little kids can give torque to bicycle
pedals, and make the wheels turn.

What factors allow things to turn easily? We know that some things turn more easily than others, but why are there these differences? When something starts to rotate or changes its rotation rate we say that it changes its "angular velocity." Because the change in velocity occurs over a period of time, it is called angular acceleration. Angular acceleration is caused by a torque, which is a force exerted at some distance from an axis of rotation.

When an unbalanced force is exerted on a mass, acceleration occurs. When you leave a stop sign in a car (which has mass), the engine exerts an unbalanced force forward to accelerate the car forward. When you brake to a stop, an unbalanced force from the brakes causes you to have a negative acceleration. When a car moves at a constant velocity, the forward force from the engine balances the backward force of friction.

An unbalanced torque produces rotational acceleration in an object. The property which resists a change in rotational motion is called "moment of inertia." In straight-line motion, acceleration is related to the force and the mass. In rotational motion, it is related to the torque and the moment of inertia. Moment of inertia is related to the mass and how far away from the axis it is.

But what do "moment of inertia" and "torque" mean? The best way to get to know more about them is to experiment. The experiments will help you to "see" what torques are and how angular acceleration occurs. Start with a simple experiment involving torques. Most people know what a force is, but few understand what a torque is. After running that experiment, you can apply what you learn about torques to learning about angular acceleration.

Experiment 1
MATERIALS AND TOOLS
pencil
ruler
modeling clay

Place the pencil on a flat surface and then place the center of the ruler on the pencil.

Roll the modeling clay into a cylinder of uniform thickness and then break it into four pieces of equal length. Each piece should have approximately the same mass. (You can use other objects instead of modeling clay, but they should not slide off the ruler.)

Place one piece of clay at one end of the ruler and then find where you must place another piece of clay to make the ruler balance.

Predict where you must place two, and then three pieces of clay if they are to balance the one piece of clay on the end. Test your hypothesis.

Torque is the product of force times distance from the axis of rotation, in this case the pencil. (Torque = force × distance from the support.) If torques are balanced, then the ruler will be balanced. Does your data support the equation?

Experiment 2
MATERIALS AND TOOLS
bicycle wheel
string
spring scale
chalk
timer
tape
various masses

PROCEDURE

Set up the bicycle wheel so that it can turn freely. You may be able to do much of this experiment by turning a bicycle upside down and using the front wheel.

Tie a string about 20 cm (10 in) long to a spoke right next to the hub.

Tie a loop in the other end of the string so you can attach a spring scale as shown in Figure 5.

Make a mark on the wheel with chalk so you can see when the wheel makes a complete revolution.

With the wheel initially at rest, exert a constant force pulling on the wheel for 2 seconds. Exert the force *at right angles to the spokes,* which means you must pull in different directions as the wheel turns. The force should turn the wheel at a reasonable rate but also allow you to exert the force for the 2 seconds without having the string get caught in the wheel. After you exert the force, immediately remove the spring scale from the string. You may have to practice to get it right.

Immediately find the time needed for two complete revolutions of the wheel. Record the force and time in a data table.

Repeat the experiment with the same force until you get consistent results and then find the average velocity

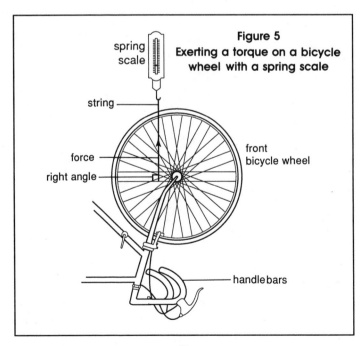

Figure 5
Exerting a torque on a bicycle wheel with a spring scale

spring scale

string

force

right angle

front bicycle wheel

handlebars

A spring scale exerts a known torque on a bicycle wheel.

by dividing the distance the wheel travels (2 revolutions in this case) by the time.

Predict what will happen when you exert twice the force or half the force for the same period of time and then test your prediction. Record your results. What happens to the angular acceleration?

Move the string so it is halfway between the rim and the hub. What is the torque now, and what do you think will happen to the angular acceleration? Test your predictions.

Put the string at other positions on the rim and see how each new position affects the way the wheel turns. Make sure that you exert the same force for the same amount of time.

Pull the string at different angles relative to the spokes. It's hard to keep the angle constant but you can do it approximately. What happens when you pull on the string in a direction parallel to the spokes?

Use tape to attach weights symmetrically around the rim of the wheel. If they are not symmetric, your wheel will not spin evenly. The weights should be heavy but still allow the wheel to turn. Taping them inside the rim may work. You have changed the moment of inertia. Now find the acceleration when you exert a torque.

What will happen when the weights are moved closer to the axis? Run the experiment and see if your answer is correct.

OTHER PROJECTS WITH ANGULAR ACCELERATION

1. When you hit a tennis ball, you don't want the racket to turn because the ball will go in an unpredictable direction. Using what you have discovered about torques and rotational motion, design a tennis racket which prevents turning. Run experiments to see if your racket is better than other rackets.

2. As a screw is screwed into a piece of wood, the torque from the screwdriver is larger than the torque from friction between the screw and the wood. After the screw is in the wood, frictional torque holds the screw in place. Design apparatus to find the torque needed to put a screw into wood and see how the torque varies for different types of screws going into different materials. Can you predict what kind of screw will be good for holding in different materials? Test your assumptions and then modify screws to make them hold better or go into the material easier.

3. A force on the pedals of a bicycle causes a torque which causes a torque in the rear wheel. The rear wheel then exerts a force on the ground to accelerate the bike. Examine differences in acceleration in the different gears.

4. Do a study of the maximum torque provided by car engines and the rates of acceleration the cars' makers advertise in their specifications. Remember, torque from the engine exerts a torque on the wheels which is the product of force times the radius of the wheels.

5. A wind exerts a torque on trees. Make models of trees of different heights and sizes to see how large a wind it takes to blow the tree over. What forces are involved and how strong does the trunk of the tree have to be to prevent snapping?

6. Sailboats must stay upright in winds. Examine the torques on sailboats when the wind blows and see what is required to keep them upright.

HOW THINGS PRECESS: OR HOW YOU RIDE A BICYCLE "NO-HANDS"

Precession of the front wheel of a bicycle allows you to ride "no-hands." When you lean, the spinning front wheel is tilted. The wheel then twists, or "precesses," just the right amount so you can turn. Some bikes seem to be easier to ride no-hands; does this mean that bicycle designers take precession into account as they build the bicycle? Is it possible to make a bicycle which can't be ridden no-hands?

Precession is caused when a rotating object wants to conserve its angular momentum. A gyroscope points in the same direction because of this. However, if you force a gyroscope or a spinning bicycle wheel to change the way it is spinning, it turns in a different way than the way you try to move it. This turning in a different way is precession. Just talking about precession instead of experimenting with it makes it hard to understand. You may also want to talk with a physics teacher who could help you get started on your investigations.

Angular momentum is related to the amount of mass of the object, how far that mass is from the axis of rotation, and how fast and in what direction the object is spinning. When you start a wheel spinning with the axis pointed vertically and then turn the axis horizontally, you change the angular momentum of the wheel. At first, there is angular momentum around the vertical axis; then it points horizontally. But angular momentum likes to be conserved! Precession occurs because the wheel tries to keep its original angular momentum and prevent a change.

This seems complicated: angular momentum, precession, and different axes. But you also know that you can ride a bicycle no-hands. How *does* precession work? The best way to find out more is to do some experiments. You can change things and investigate how those changes affect the motion. The experiment is rather simple so give it a try.

MATERIALS AND TOOLS
bicycle wheel
rope or twine that can easily support the bicycle wheel
chalk
timer
weights

Gyroscopes make use of the principle of conservation of angular momentum. They are used in the inertial guidance systems of missiles and air- and spacecraft.

PROCEDURE

Caution: In conducting this experiment, be careful not to get your fingers caught in the spokes. *It hurts!*

Take a wheel off a bicycle and tie the rope to one end of the axle as in Figure 6. Make sure the rope will not slip off.

Put a mark on the wheel with the chalk so you can see how fast the wheel is spinning when you turn it.

Start the wheel spinning with the axle pointed horizontally, and hold the rope so that the wheel can move freely. If the wheel is spinning fast enough, it will not fall immediately. The motion you observe is called precession. Record your observations.

Spin the wheel again and find how many revolutions it makes in 10 seconds. Record this value.

Now, spin it the way you just did and time how long it takes for the wheel to precess, or spin on another axis, one complete revolution. Record this time.

What will happen if you spin the wheel faster or slower? Test your hypothesis. Record all your data.

The gravitational force on the wheel has been providing a torque which causes the precession (see previous section on torques). Tie weights to a string attached to the side of the wheel opposite from where you are supporting the wheel. What happens to the precession rate? What happens when you spin the wheel in the opposite direction?

What will happen if the mass of the wheel is changed? Tape weights symmetrically at the rim so the wheel will spin evenly. What happens to the precession rate?

OTHER PROJECTS WITH PRECESSION

1. Modify the angle the front fork holding the front wheel of a bicycle makes relative to the vertical. **(Be careful not to hurt yourself or damage the bike.)** Can you still ride

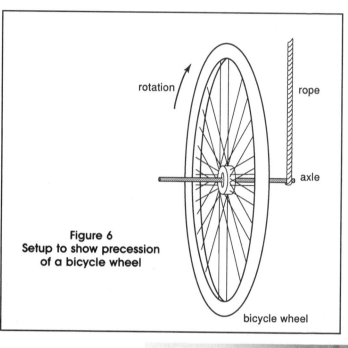

rotation

rope

axle

**Figure 6
Setup to show precession
of a bicycle wheel**

bicycle wheel

A spinning bicycle
wheel, supported
by one side of the
axle, demonstrates
the principle of
precession.

no-hands? Is it possible to make a bicycle which can't be ridden because of precession?

2. Experiment with a frisbee and see how the direction changes with the way the frisbee tilts. Does the amount of mass at the rim make a difference? What is the ideal placement of the mass to keep the frisbee going straight? What happens with different spin rates, or when you spin the frisbee in the opposite direction?

3. Make a model of a hard disk drive for a computer. (Get the mass and rotation rate from the specifications.) Then examine the forces acting on the axle of the drive when the computer is bumped, forcing the "wheel" to tip.

4. Experiment with the rotation rate of a football and how it changes the direction the ball points during flight. Experiment with different rotation rates.

5. Design and build a rotating wheel you can place in a suitcase or similar enclosure. Then, walk with the suitcase and see what your friends think. The precession of the wheel in the suitcase will cause it to behave *very* strangely. You may want to use an electric motor to keep the wheel spinning.

OTHER PROJECTS IN MECHANICS

1. Flags flap in the air. Experiment with flags of different sizes and shapes to see if they flap at different rates. Can you design a flag that flaps at a particular rate? How are flags like leaves fluttering in the wind?

2. Experiment with a bicycle on a hill to find the best shape for reducing air friction. What position should you take? What can you build to reduce air friction?

3. Make a study of driving nails into different kinds of wood with different types of hammers. Which are the most effective? What shape nail goes in easiest?

4. Make a study of the distance an arrow flies from a bow when the bow is stretched different amounts. **(Do this**

only with permission from a responsible adult.) What happens when different bows are used?

5. Examine the skipping of stones. How do spin, shape, and velocity affect the number of skips.

6. How do boomerangs come back? Analyze the forces and rotation of the boomerang. How do size, shape, and rotation rate affect them?

7. Two pendulums swinging side by side and tied to the same horizontal support can trade energy. (These are called coupled pendulums.) Start one swinging, and the other will start as the first stops. Start with pendulums of equal length and then try others of unequal length.

8. How do you swing on a swing? What effect would wearing heavy shoes have? What about the length of the ropes? How do you increase the height at which you are swinging?

FOR FURTHER READING

American Association of Physics Teachers. *Physics of Sports.* College Park, Md.: American Association of Physics Teachers, 1986.

Gardner, Robert. *Science and Sports.* New York: Franklin Watts, 1988.

Goodwin, Peter. *Engineering Projects for Young Scientists.* New York: Franklin Watts, 1987.

Hosking, Wayne. *Flights of Imagination.* Washington, D.C.: National Science Teachers Association, 1987.

4

THE MOLECULAR WORLD: SMALL THINGS IN MOTION

Thermodynamics is the study of how molecules exchange heat and how they affect one another. The motion of molecules is related to their temperature, and they are always in motion.

Because water is familiar to us, it is a good example of how substances exist in different states. We often see water as a solid, a liquid, or a gas. Each state has distinctive properties, and water exists in one state or the other depending on temperature. Ice has rigid bonds so it is solid. Liquid water has fewer rigid bonds so it flows, but the molecules still like to hold on to one another and form drops. Water in the vapor stage is called steam or just water vapor. Water vapor can exist at temperatures below the boiling point, and when there is a lot of it in the air, we say that it is humid.

Experiments investigating how atoms behave are very helpful in making thermodynamics understandable. The experiments help you to visualize what the invisible molecules are doing and to get a better feel for how they behave. Microscopes used in a biology class allow you to see objects made of many molecules. Even the leg of a microscopic bug has many, many molecules. The experiments which follow should help you to understand what the individual molecules do and how they behave. As you do the experiments, try to relate the effects you see to what the molecules are doing.

As with the section on mechanics, this section gives a few starting experiments and then suggests a few advanced experiments. These are by no means the only experiments you can do. A scientist works by asking questions, so these experiments may lead to other experiments.

Remember to have fun, but be careful as you make your measurements and observations. Record your data carefully so you can check your results. If you make mistakes in your procedure or in taking data, you may end up with inaccurate results which, in turn, may lead to incorrect conclusions.

MOLECULES: A FEW
INTRODUCTORY EXPERIMENTS

Molecules fit together in different ways because of the different types of molecular bonds. Often, spaces exist between the molecules where other molecules can fit. You can add salt to water, for instance, and the volume changes much less than the volume of salt you add.

But how much space is there between molecules? How can you measure the amount of space? A few quick, simple experiments might be of help.

Experiment 1
MATERIALS AND TOOLS
two measuring cups
dry sand
water

PROCEDURE

Fill one measuring cup half full of dry sand, and the other half full of water. Record the measurements.

Add the water to the sand a little at a time. After adding some water, wait until it sinks into the sand before adding more. Stop adding water when no more soaks into the sand.

Measure the amount of water left in the measuring cup, and calculate the amount that soaked into the sand. Does this amount surprise you? Where did it go? What does this mean about the sand?

Experiment 2

MATERIALS AND TOOLS
two measuring cups
warm water
granulated sugar

PROCEDURE

Fill one measuring cup half full of the warm water, and the other half full of the sugar. Record the two volumes.

Add a little bit of sugar to the water and stir it until it dissolves completely. Measure the volume of sugar left in the measuring cup and the new volume of the sugar water. Record these values.

Keep adding sugar to the water a little at a time. Each time you add sugar, record the amount of sugar left (so you can calculate the volume you added) and the volume of the sugar water.

Keep adding sugar even when you can't make it dissolve until you have added your half cup of sugar.

For each time you added sugar, calculate the volume of sugar that you added (from the start) and the total change in volume of the sugar water. What do you observe?

How is this experiment similar to or different from Experiment 1? Do different things happen to the volume of the sugar water after you can't dissolve all the sugar in the water?

Experiment 3
MATERIALS AND TOOLS
large pan
water
fine sawdust
eyedropper
dishwashing soap (liquid)
meterstick

PROCEDURE
Fill a large pan (such as a baking pan) half full with water as in Figure 7. Sprinkle the sawdust over the surface of the water.

Use the eyedropper to form a drop of the liquid soap. Measure the diameter of this drop as precisely as possible.

Release the drop into the center of the pan. You should see the sawdust move away from the point where it hits.

Measure the area of the region where the soap pushed the sawdust away as precisely as possible.

Calculate the volume of the drop using the drop's radius. Then using the area of the region cleared of sawdust, calculate the thickness of the soap film (volume = area × thickness). This thickness approximates the diameter of a molecule of soap.

Does the size of the soap molecule (which is much bigger than a water molecule) surprise you?

**OTHER PROJECTS
WITH MOLECULES**

1. Try adding other substances to water and see how the volume of the water changes when a given volume of the

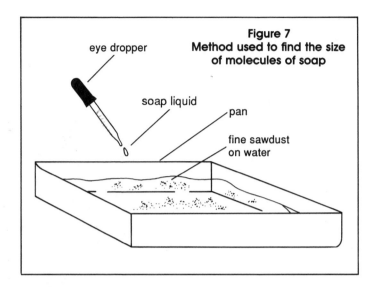

Figure 7
**Method used to find the size
of molecules of soap**

eye dropper

soap liquid

pan

fine sawdust
on water

substance is added. **Make sure an adult says that adding your substance is OK. Some substances are dangerous, and others are either very expensive or will make a mess.** You might start with salt and salad oil.

2. Repeat Experiment 1 on p. 52 using different types of dry sand or gravel to see if there's a difference in the amount of water you can add. Also, try adding water to other objects of different shapes.

3. Experiment to see how changing the temperature of water changes the amount of sugar which will dissolve in it.

HOW HEAT FLOWS: HEAT LOSS AND INSULATION

Heat, or thermal energy, is transferred when the kinetic energy of molecules is given from one molecule to another. Some materials conduct heat well while others conduct it poorly. Whether a material is a good conductor or a poor conductor often has to do with how far apart the molecules of the substance are. If it is hard for a molecule of the substance to hit another molecule and give away some energy, it is harder for the substance to conduct heat.

But what causes the difference in heat conduction? Why do you keep warm in the clothes you wear, and why do some of them lose their insulating ability if they get wet? What happens if the heated molecules can leave the area by convection? Does evaporation play a part in cooling? Why might Styrofoam cups and pieces of metal have different rates of conduction? Can things with the density of metals conduct heat as poorly as Styrofoam?

Answering some of these questions can be fun. Experimenting with how heat travels through different materials can also help you understand what makes good insulators or bad ones. It can help you to understand how you can insulate a house and make it energy efficient. You can also start to think about how different animals survive in different situations.

The experiment outlined below examines different kinds of insulation and which insulations will keep water hot for longer periods of time. Develop a hypothesis about the results, and then run the experiment to check whether your hypothesis is correct.

MATERIALS AND TOOLS
various containers of similar shape such as Styrofoam, metal,
    glass, and paper cups
measuring cup
hot water
thermometer
covers (such as file cards) for the containers
watch with a second hand

Take one of your containers and use the measuring cup to fill it half full with hot water from a faucet. **Make sure that you don't get scalded by the water.** Record the amount of water that you add to your container.

Measure and record the temperature of the water. (Allow the thermometer to adjust to the final temperature. It may take half a minute or so.)

Cover the container with a lid. After 2 minutes have passed, find the temperature again. Continue recording the time and the temperature at 2-minute intervals until 10 minutes have passed. Then set the container aside and find the temperature 10 minutes later. At the end, your data should show the temperature initially, and at 2, 4, 6, 8, 10, and 20 minutes.

Repeat your measurements for the other containers. Test to see the difference when there is a cover on the container as compared to no cover. (It may be possible to measure the temperatures of more than one container at a time. You need about half a minute to find each temperature and you take temperatures every 2 minutes.)

Plot graphs of the temperature versus time for your containers (time on the horizontal axis) and see if the cooling rates agree with what you expected.

Run other experiments to answer the following questions:

- What effect does a lid have on the container?

- What happens if you use two or three Styrofoam cups, one inside the other, to increase the thickness of the insulation?

- What happens to the cooling rate as time goes by?

- Is heat being lost at a different rate at the end of the 20 minutes?

As you run these experiments, make sure that you don't change more than one variable at a time. Otherwise, you will not be able to draw proper conclusions.

Do the results of your experiment agree with what you expected? Does the density of the material seem to indicate the rate at which heat flows through it? What must be happening on the molecular level?

OTHER PROJECTS
WITH INSULATION

1. All objects in a room are at the same temperature, but some of them "feel" cooler than others. Examine various materials and see if some feel cooler than others. Does the experiment described above help you to explain the differences you feel?

2. Using a larger container of water (such as a picnic cooler or large pot), find if the beginning experiment works with larger quantities of water and larger surface areas. You may have to take the temperature at longer time intervals in order to see the changes.

3. Examine the difference between something warming up and something cooling down by starting with cold water instead of warm. Do you expect a difference? Is there any?

4. Insulation changes its properties when wet. Run an experiment to see what happens when fiberglass housing insulation is "wet" with differing amounts of water. What does your experiment tell you about the need to keep fiber glass insulation dry? What happens to the insulating properties of down or other materials used in sleeping bags when they are wet? Which materials seem to be the best when wet? Would this be a reason to buy this kind of insulation?

5. Run experiments to find the temperature of a damp object when a fan blows air over it. Does the humidity of the air affect your results? Could you design an air conditioner which worked on this principle?

6. Experiment with different building materials and see how well they insulate. Which are going to be the best at keeping heat in? (R values tell us something about this, but your experiments may tell more.)

7. Find two houses similar in size and find how they are insulated. Then compare the amount of energy the houses use during the winter. (It will help if they both use the same kind of fuel, such as oil or gas.) How does the insulation affect the heat loss? What other factors make a difference in the amount of heat lost by a house during the heating season? You may also have to think about how much cold air sneaks into the house through cracks (called infiltration). Drafty houses with cracks around the windows and doors need more heat, too.

SOLAR HEATING: HOW TO TRAP THE SUN'S ENERGY

Solar energy is free but it takes money to build the device which collects it. Finding economical ways to collect this nonpolluting energy source is important for the world, but what kind of collector is the most economical for a given situation? How much energy can you collect during a day? Can solar energy collectors be simple enough to build so that even people in developing nations can build them?

A few experiments with solar energy collectors can help you find answers to these questions. You may have some idea of what will make a good collector, but are your hunches correct? By looking at the cost of the model collector and how much energy it collects, you can figure if it is worth the cost of building the actual collector.

As you do these experiments, think of modifications which will make energy collection more efficient. However, you should be realistic about building a large-scale collector. Can you make your collector large enough to heat a house or the hot water for a house or would it be unreliable? It is easier to collect energy in the summer than in the winter, but does this affect whether your collector would be good for heating a house or hot water?

MATERIALS AND TOOLS

two similar baking pans

water

thermometer

piece of aluminum foil (to cover the inside bottom surface of one pan)

piece of black plastic (to cover the inside bottom surface of the other pan)

piece of glass (to cover the top of one pan)

PROCEDURE

Fill both baking pans with water of the same temperature. Find and record this initial temperature.

Cut the pieces of aluminum foil and black plastic so each will cover the inside bottom surface of a pan.

Place the aluminum foil in the bottom of one pan and the black plastic in the bottom of the other as shown in Figure 8. Small weights or a small amount of sand may be needed to keep the plastic on the bottom.

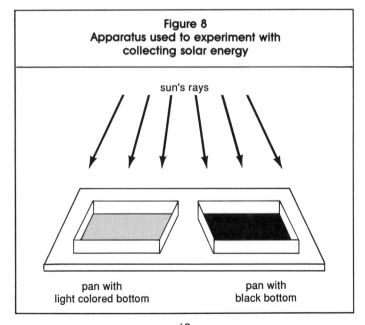

Figure 8
Apparatus used to experiment with collecting solar energy

sun's rays

pan with
light colored bottom

pan with
black bottom

Place both pans in the sun for 5 minutes; then find the temperature of the water in both pans and record the values.

Let the pans stay in the sun another 5 minutes and check the temperatures again. Which solar collector seems to collect heat the best?

Repeat your experiment, starting with water at the same temperature, but put the piece of glass over one of the pans. How does the temperature of the pan with the cover change with time? Did you expect this?

OTHER PROJECTS WITH
SOLAR COLLECTORS

1. Change the material in the bottom of the pans in the beginning experiment to see if other materials collect more heat. You might try different colors such as blue, green, or red. If red materials seem to absorb heat better, try different red materials.

2. Design a collector with reflectors that focus more sunlight on it. Does the water heat twice as fast when you reflect light from twice the area?

3. Examine what happens if winds are blowing across the pan of water. You might need a fan to provide a "constant" wind for a "controlled" experiment.

4. Examine what happens when more than one layer of glass is used to cover the pan. Does the angle at which the sun's rays hit the cover affect your result?

5. Design a system with a pump which will allow you to tilt the collector and have the water flow across the surface. Does this system collect more heat? Is it worth the extra cost of a pump?

6. Design a way to measure the amount of heat collected over the course of a day with a given kind of collector. Compare it to other collectors and try to find the most efficient design for daylong energy collection.

HOW THINGS FLOAT: BUOYANCY
AND ARCHIMEDES' PRINCIPLE

Quite obviously, some things float while others sink. If the downward force of gravity is larger than the upward force from the fluid, be it water, mercury, or air, the object will sink. Most objects "sink" in air because the density of air is very small, but lots of things float on mercury because its density is almost fourteen times that of water. In a sea of mercury a boat could carry almost fourteen times its normal cargo.

Objects float because the upward force on the object's bottom, the buoyant force, equals gravity. When this happens, gravity and the buoyant force balance, so the net force is zero. The object does not accelerate up or down.

The gravitational force on an object can be measured easily but what affects the upward force on an object's bottom? Why does a boat sink farther into the water as it is loaded with cargo? Why do some people float in the water and others sink? Why is it easier to float in the ocean than in fresh water? Why do rocks feel lighter when lifted in water and heavier when you lift them out of the water?

In trying to answer these questions, it may help to know the equation for water pressure. You probably have experienced an increase in pressure with depth. You feel more pressure on the bottom of a swimming pool. The actual equation states: $P = \rho g d$, where P is the pressure in N (newtons)/m^2, ρ is the density of the fluid in kg/m^3, g is the acceleration of gravity in m/sec^2 and is about 10 on the surface of the Earth, and d is the depth in meters.

Examine the equation and the buoyant force by running the simple experiment which follows. You may find that some of your ideas about floating are correct while others are not. Try to think about why things happen. Remember, it is the difference in pressure which causes buoyant force. If part of an object is submerged, pressure pushes down on the top as well as up on the bottom. However, if it floats, the upward force can be large enough to equal the gravitational force.

MATERIALS AND TOOLS
various masses of different densities
light, strong thread or string
spring scale
pitcher with straight sides holding 2 quarts (1.9 liters) or more
  of water
wooden stick slightly shorter than the pitcher is tall
meterstick
pen

PROCEDURE
Take a mass and tie some thread or string to it. The thread or string should weigh much less than the object. Tie a loop in the thread so you can attach it to the spring scale to find the weight. Record the weight.

Lower the object into a pitcher of water until it is covered with water or the string exerts no force, as in Figure 9. (This happens if the object floats on its own.)

Find the new force exerted on the spring scale and record it. If the object floats, it will be zero.

Repeat your procedure with the other objects you have found. Include metal, wood, rubber, and hollow objects. Make a hypothesis about whether each object will float or not before you run the experiment.

Now, take the wooden stick and, with the pen, make marks every 10 cm and label these marks.

Tie string to the stick and then find the weight using the spring scale.

Lower the stick into the pitcher and find the weight at each mark. Does moving the stick twice as far into the water cause twice the upward force from water pressure? Does this make sense according to the equation for water pressure?

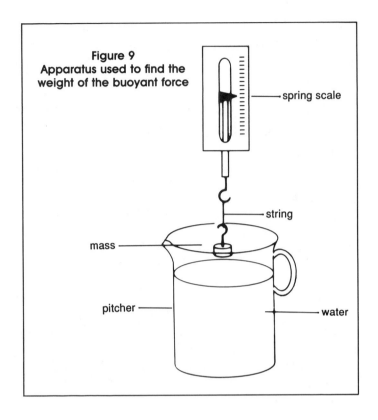

Figure 9
Apparatus used to find the weight of the buoyant force

- spring scale
- string
- mass
- pitcher
- water

OTHER PROJECTS WITH BUOYANCY

1. Experiment with liquids of different densities, such as sugar water. **Use *clean*, nonpoisonous objects** such as two jars with weights in the bottom. One jar should float, and the other should sink rapidly. Each must weigh less than the maximum weight your spring scale can measure. Draw a line at the waterline where the floating object floats, and find the weight of the sinking object in water. Then add ice tea mix or another drink containing sugar to the water.

Add it in four equal amounts, each time measuring where the waterline is on the floating jar and how much the sinking jar weighs. What changes do you note? You may want to add other things to the pitcher and see what differences they make, but don't drink the content.

2. Make a hydrometer, a device which can tell the density of a liquid, by filling one end of a small tube with some sand. Float the hydrometer in water and mark with a pencil or pen where the water line is. Find the density of water by dividing a mass of a certain volume of water by the volume. Mark the water level on the tube with this density. Now, add sugar or salt to the water to change the density of the water, find the density, and mark the tube. Repeat this a couple of times and then you can use your hydrometer to find unknown densities. Hydrometers can be used to see if there is enough antifreeze in a car's cooling system.

3. Build a model of a submarine by using a plastic soda bottle and a small rubber tube. Put some sand into the bottle. Make two holes in the cap and stick the rubber tube in one. By blowing air in or sucking it out you can make the bottle float or sink.

4. Fill a container full with water and see how the weight of the water which overflows when an object is put into the water compares to the change in weight of the object.

5. Some people float and some sink. Some are sort of in the middle and float with full lungs but sink if they exhale. Examine how they float at certain times and sink at others. What do they do to increase the upward force so they float? If they make a bubble of air in their swimsuit, how does this help them to float?

6. At a swimming pool, tie a weight onto a clean soda bottle. Make it so that the combined weight and bottle just float. Then, lower them into the pool. What do you think will happen? What causes the actual result?

HOW TEMPERATURE AFFECTS
LIQUIDS AND SOLIDS:
EXPANSION AND CONTRACTION

Expansion of liquids and solids as temperature changes is sometimes a problem and sometimes useful. Materials that expand or contract at different rates can cause structures to break. Pipes bursting when water freezes in them is an example. However, the fact that materials expand and contract with changes in temperature is used to make thermometers, thermostats, and similar devices.

But how much do things expand or contract when their temperature changes? Do different substances expand or contract different amounts? Do they expand or contract different amounts at different temperatures?

Experimenting to find the answers to these questions can be fun. You can also begin to understand what problems scientists face as they design containers to hold liquids. If cold gasoline is pumped into a car's gas tank on a warm day, the gas will eventually warm up to air temperature. But if the gas expands too much, it overflows and causes atmospheric pollution. How can scientists design the tanks to avoid this problem? Likewise, a bridge crossing a river must be designed so it still crosses the river with a change in temperature. How can the bridge be built so it is safe?

Start your investigation by thinking about what you know about things expanding with temperature changes and then run simple experiments to test your hunches. After you do these experiments, you may want to work on some further experiments to test other hypotheses. Remember, plan your experiments carefully and take your data carefully. Otherwise, you may draw incorrect conclusions.

Experiment 1
MATERIALS AND TOOLS
Pyrex flask with a volume of about 500 ml

cold water from a faucet
thermometer
two-holed stopper
glass tubing, about 30 cm
meterstick

Fill the flask with water.

Be careful as you do the next two steps because if you break glass, you can injure yourself.

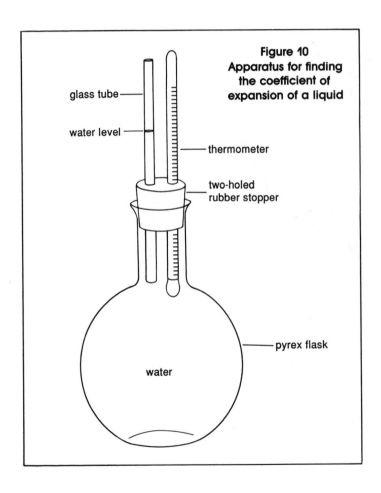

Figure 10
Apparatus for finding
the coefficient of
expansion of a liquid

glass tube

water level

thermometer

two-holed
rubber stopper

pyrex flask

water

Insert the thermometer into the stopper. Lubricating the thermometer with glycerin may make it easier to push it in. Then insert the glass tubing into the stopper. Again, glycerin may make it slide in more easily.

Note: If you use glycerin, make sure that you take your apparatus apart after you use it to prevent it from sticking.

Now insert the stopper into the flask filled with water as in Figure 10. Water should be pushed up the tube about 2 cm (1 in) above the stopper when the stopper is in place. You may have to make a few attempts before you get the water to reach the proper level.

Wait until the thermometer reads a constant value. Record this value in a data table.

Measure the distance the water is up the tube from the stopper. Record this value.

Now, hold the flask in your hands until the temperature rises 5 degrees Celsius. Record the new temperature and the distance the water has been pushed up the tube. **Do not hold the flask over a direct heat source.**

Keep raising the temperature in 5-degree intervals by holding the flask in your hands until you can't raise it any more. Record your data.

Draw a graph of temperature versus distance the water has been pushed up the tube. What does this tell you about the expansion of water?

Experiment 2
MATERIALS AND TOOLS
rubber hose
piece of rubber tubing, 2 cm (1 in) long
piece of metal tubing between .5 and 1 m long
funnel
stand
scissors
some cardboard
protractor
pen

needle
water
bucket
ice

PROCEDURE

Attach the rubber hose to one end of the metal tubing and the other end to the narrow part of the funnel. Place the funnel in the stand so it won't fall over.

Place the small piece of rubber tubing over the other end of the tube.

With the scissors, cut a disk out of cardboard and then use the protractor to mark the disk to 360 degrees, marking every tenth degree. Push the needle through the center of the cardboard disk, making sure the disk is balanced and turns on its own.

Place the apparatus near a table edge with the needle under the small section of rubber tubing. Place the bucket so it will catch the water that flows through the tube, as in Figure 11.

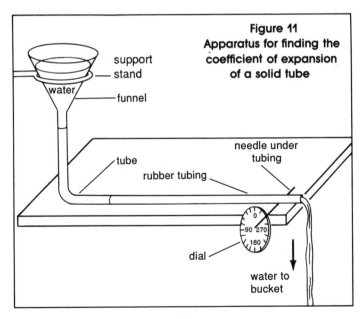

Figure 11
Apparatus for finding the coefficient of expansion of a solid tube

support
stand
water
funnel
tube
rubber tubing
needle under tubing
dial
water to bucket

Notice the position of the disk and then pour ice water into the funnel so it flows through the tubing. This will lower the temperature of the tube. The disk should turn. Record the amount that the disk turns and which way.

Now pour hot water through the tube and record the results. Do your results agree with what you expected?

OTHER PROJECTS WITH EXPANSION AND CONTRACTION

1. Instead of cold water in Experiment 1, try ice chips in a flask to reduce the temperature to 0° Celsius (32° Fahrenheit). **Do not place a water-filled flask in a freezer because you may break the flask.** Repeat the experiment as you warm up the flask with your hands. What does your data show?

2. Place your flask in a pot of boiling water **(make sure the flask is no longer cold, and be careful not to burn yourself)**, and see how water expands at higher temperatures. **Do not hold the flask over a direct heat source.** Find the coefficient of expansion by dividing the change in volume of the liquid (the cross-sectional area of the tube times the distance the water moves) by the total volume of the liquid.

3. Take data for the water temperature and the dial position in project 2 above and draw a graph of temperature versus amount of expansion. Use a few different tubing materials such as copper, aluminum, glass, and steel and observe the differences. You may want to calculate the "coefficient of linear expansion," which is the amount of expansion divided by the length of the tube and the temperature change ($\Delta l/(L \times \Delta T)$). Find the change in length by using the circumference of the pin and the amount the disk turns.

4. Attach strips of two different types of metal together with bolts at either end and one in the middle. See if you

can predict the changes that occur. Can you make this device into a switch which turns a flashlight on and off?

5. Make a thermometer which uses a flask of water (you might add food coloring) and a small tube. See how well it behaves as compared to one bought in a store. You might add antifreeze to a thermometer so it can measure temperatures below freezing. **Be careful with the antifreeze. It's poisonous and must not come into contact with food or drinks.**

6. Given that both solids and liquids expand or contract with temperature, try to predict the exact amount of expansion of water in a container given that the container increases its volume, too. Does your prediction agree with the actual result?

SURFACE TENSION: ITS STRENGTH AND EFFECT

Surface tension is caused by the molecules on the surface holding together more strongly than the molecules under the surface. For this reason, surface tension tends to pull liquids into spheres because spheres have the smallest surface area for a given volume. Soap bubbles are very spherical for this reason. Surface tension also allows bugs to stay on the surface of the water.

We all know surface tension exists, but how strong a force is it? How can it be changed? Is it the same for all kinds of liquids? Experiments with surface tension can help you to answer these questions. You may be able to understand how it is possible to "float" a razor blade on water and how you can sink it without touching it.

As you start this experiment, you may not know what questions to ask. However, after doing the experiment you may find that questions start to develop and that these questions will lead you to other experiments of your own. Work carefully and you may discover something.

MATERIALS AND TOOLS
baking pan
water
fine wire
sensitive spring scale
liquid dishwashing soap
eyedropper

PROCEDURE

Fill a small baking pan half full with water.

Take some fine wire and make a small loop which can be hung on the spring scale. Make a vertical section and then a loop which will be in the water. (The wire should be small in diameter, and bare speaker wire should work. If the speaker wire is made from a number of smaller wires, you might use one of the smaller wires.)

The spring scale must be able to measure differences in force of 1/1000 of a newton (about 1/10 of a gram).

Use the spring scale to find the weight of the wire when it is out of the water. Record this value.

Lower the wire into the water and then find the force on the spring scale as you remove the wire. Record the maximum value. The difference between the first reading and the second is the surface tension force.

Change the shape and length of the section of wire which goes into the water and observe the changes in surface tension force. Does the force double when the length of the wire in the water is doubled? Are any shapes of wire capable of causing more force?

Add the liquid dishwashing soap to the water a drop at a time from the eyedropper and observe the changes in the force required to remove the wire from the water.

OTHER PROJECTS WITH SURFACE TENSION

1. Surface tension makes the surface area of the liquid the

smallest possible. See how the soap film connects wire formed into loops of different shapes and see if it always chooses the smallest surface area. Try making a wire cube or triangle. What happens to the film?

2. Take data so that you can make a graph of the surface tension versus the amount of soap added to the water. Does adding more soap always change the surface tension?

3. Examine the effects of other kinds of soap or other substances on the surface tension of water. **Make sure to use only *safe* substances which have been approved by an adult. Some chemicals around the house are quite dangerous to work with.**

4. Examine the shapes of water drops sitting on a surface like waxed paper. How is their shape related to their size?

5. Many books exist on how to make soap bubbles. They have different recommendations for how to make the bubble mixtures. Can you find a better mixture for making bubbles? Is the mixture different if you want to make large bubbles? If you want to make bubbles that last a long time?

HOW AIRPLANES FLY:
THE BERNOULLI EFFECT

The Bernoulli effect explains a number of things, such as how airplanes fly, how can you draw water up a straw by blowing across the top, and why you can suspend a Ping-Pong ball in the airstream from a hair drier (don't use heat or you may melt the ball). This effect occurs because the pressure of a fluid—a gas or liquid—is dependent on how fast the fluid is going. The faster it moves, the lower the pressure.

But how large is this force and when does it occur? Can it occur with all gases? What about a wing in the water? Is there a Bernoulli force in this case?

Some experiments involving the Bernoulli force are simple to run but measuring the actual forces can require precise measurement. Run a few simple experiments and then see if you want to take the time to get precise data. However you start your experiments, start by asking questions, then test your hunches and make sure that you enjoy yourself.

MATERIALS AND TOOLS
paper
tape
stopwatch

Take a paper strip about 3 cm wide and 10 cm long (1 in × 4 in) and hold it just above your mouth. Blow out through your mouth and observe the result.

Now, place the strip just below your mouth. Predict the result of blowing out and then test your hypothesis.

Try blowing at different speeds and see what happens.

Blow over the paper at a constant speed and get it to move a certain amount. Blowing at this constant rate, time how long it takes to empty your lungs after you inhale as deeply as you can.

Then, tape another piece of paper the same size on top of the first. This will approximately double the weight. Blow over the top of the paper and get the double strip to move in the same way as before. What happens to the rate you have to blow? Time how long it takes to exhale at this rate and compare the velocity at which the air is traveling to produce twice the force.

Repeat the experiment with more and more sheets until you can't blow fast enough.

Caution: **Be careful that you don't hyperventilate (breathe too much for the amount of work you are doing) in the process. If you start to feel dizzy, take a break from your experiment before you continue.**

OTHER PROJECTS WITH
THE BERNOULLI EFFECT

The problem with doing more experiments is that the forces involved are small and the actual speed at which the fluids move is hard to measure. You can solve these problems, but you may need help and equipment from a science lab.

1. Use a vacuum cleaner with the hose on the air outlet as an air source. Have this airstream go past a flat object like a small piece of cardboard. Use a sensitive spring scale to measure the force. Vary the speed the air is moving past the cardboard and see how the force varies with the angle, speed, and size of the cardboard.

2. Run a similar experiment to project 1 but use water instead of air. Hydrofoils "fly" through the water by using underwater wings like airplane wings.

3. Set up a large water supply such as a bucket and use the siphon effect and a T-tube to examine pressure changes with velocity. Rubber hose can be used to make the water flow out of the bucket and then through the T-tube and then finally to another bucket. Measure the flow rate by measuring how fast the lower bucket fills up. You can vary the flow rate by pinching the tube with a clamp.

4. Examine the forces on a Ping-Pong ball in the airflow of a hair dryer. What determines the force exerted on the ball? What happens if the mass of the ball is changed? What happens if the size is changed? Can you change the way the air leaves the hair dryer to get a better effect? *Remember,* don't use heat from the hair dryer or you may melt your Ping-Pong ball.

OTHER PROJECTS IN
THERMODYNAMICS

1. Investigate how the size of a balloon changes as you lower it into a swimming pool.

**The Bernoulli effect: a ball in the air is
suspended by the exhaust of a vacuum cleaner.**

2. Snowflakes form different types of crystals under different circumstances. Allow them to land on a surface which is below the freezing point. Then, keep a log of the types of snow that fall and the conditions that generate the flakes. (Drawing diagrams of the flakes will help you to remember their shapes.) Remember, air temperatures may be different in air layers above where you see the snowflakes.

3. Examine how cooling air produces clouds. A simple example is exhaling on a cool day. Design an experiment to examine the amount of cooling needed to get air containing different amounts of water vapor to form clouds. Relate this to cloud formation in the atmosphere.

4. Run an experiment to see how a metal skewer can make meat cook faster. How large should the skewers be and how should they be placed for the most efficient cooking?

5. Make a study of the climate associated with a mountain range which crosses the normal wind flow. (The Sierra Nevada Mountains are a good example.) What happens to the air as it rises and then descends? What does this do to the climate of the area?

6. Examine how snowballs form. When you compress them, some ice melts for a moment and then refreezes. What different conditions produce the best snowballs? What conditions make it very hard to make them at all?

7. Drops of water on a fry pan will often bounce for long periods of time. Run experiments to see what temperature is best and what conditions help a drop to last as long as possible. An electric fry pan with a thermostat will make this experiment easier. *Caution:* **The hot surface can burn you. Be careful.**

FOR FURTHER READING

Atkins, P. W. *The Second Law.* New York: W. H. Freeman, 1984.

5

VIBRATIONS AND ELECTROMAGNETISM

Vibrations, electricity, and magnetism are related in some ways but different in others. The kind of electricity we use most often is alternating current. This electric current occurs as electric fields cause charges to vibrate back and forth. Current in a light bulb moves back and forth as the electric fields make it go one way and then the other. Photons are electromagnetic radiation and include visible light, ultraviolet radiation, X rays, microwaves, and radio waves.

Photons cause things to vibrate as they pass by. Radio waves cause charges in a radio antenna to move, and this motion is then amplified to produce sound. Microwave ovens cook food because they give energy to water molecules in the food. The microwave frequency causes the water molecules to rotate rapidly one way and then the other. The frequency is one of the "natural frequencies" of the water molecules so they vibrate at that rate. This vibrating motion is transferred to the other atoms around the water molecules and heats them up. Physicists have found that magnetic force is actually caused by the electric forces so they are actually the same force.

On a larger scale, a person can make a swing move higher and higher by putting in energy at the right time, at the "natural frequency" of the swing. If you put energy in at a frequency other than the natural frequency, you will not make the swing go higher and higher.

When experimenting with waves and electromagnetism, try to think about what will happen before you do the experiment. Your initial guess may be wrong, but you learn from your mistakes. Be careful as you run the experiment because incorrect data can cause you to draw incorrect conclusions. Have fun but be careful to get good data as well as collect your data safely.

HOW THINGS BOUNCE: WHAT AFFECTS THE PERIOD OF MOTION?

We often see things vibrating. When a car goes over a bump, it bounces for a while until the shock absorbers stop the motion. A guitar string vibrates after it is plucked and produces sounds as it slows down. Trees sway to and fro in a wind with a characteristic frequency, with the smaller trees having different frequencies from large ones.

Is the vibration frequency something you can predict? Is it related to something characteristic of the thing which vibrates? Experiments can help you to understand the way things vibrate and see why they vibrate at different frequencies. Big objects seem to vibrate at lower frequencies than smaller ones, but why? Is it always so or are there exceptions?

The frequency at which things vibrate is determined by two things: the mass of the object and the amount of force which returns it to its equilibrium point, or point where forces are balanced. A guitar string normally is straight, and the forces on it are balanced. When it's plucked, it's moved away from its equilibrium position, but a force tends to make it move back toward that position again. If the string is pulled tighter, a larger force accelerates the string's mass with a larger acceleration, causing a faster vibration. On a much smaller scale, the vibration frequency of a water molecule in microwaves is related to the mass of the molecule and the force causing the acceleration. Because of their small mass, the water molecules vibrate millions of times a second!

You can run simple experiments with vibrations easily. Some investigations, however, may require more equipment but may allow you to understand more about why and how things vibrate. Before you start your experiments, try to think about what the results might be and compare your guess to the actual results. If your guess is right, then you learn something. If it's wrong, you learn something too.

MATERIALS AND TOOLS
rubber bands
two supports
small weights (a few pens or pencils will do)
tape
timer

PROCEDURE
Stretch a rubber band between two supports which won't move when you stretch the rubber band.

Attach a small weight to the center of the rubber band. Use tape to make sure that the weight stays attached when the band moves.

Pull the weight down and release it. Time how long it takes for 10 cycles (the time it takes to move up and down ten times). If it bounces up and down too fast to record the time, either start with two or more weights or reduce the tension in the rubber band. Record the time for 10 cycles, the number of weights, and the approximate tension of the rubber band.

Repeat your measurement to get a second value, record it, and then find the average value for time. Use this to find the time for 1 cycle.

Repeat the experiment adding one then two more weights.

Experiment using more than one rubber band.

Now, change the tension in the rubber band and see what happens.

OTHER PROJECTS WITH VIBRATING OBJECTS

1. Find out what factors affect the period of a mass bouncing on the end of a spring or combination of springs.

2. Take a long board such as one 1 in × 4 in × 8 ft (2.5 cm × 10 cm × 2.4 m) and attach it firmly with clamps to a solid table so about 2 feet (.6 m) of it is on the table and the other 6 feet (1.8 m) are in the air. **(Be careful not to damage the table.)** Push down on the board and find the period of vibration. Change the amount hanging off the table and see how the vibration rate changes. The movement of this board is very much like that of a diving board in use or the up-and-down motion of an airplane wing as the plane flies. How do designers plan for this kind of bouncing?

3. Experiment with a pogo stick and see if it is possible to change the rate at which the stick bounces up and down. Is the rate the same for all people who use the stick? What could you do to change the period of the pogo stick?

4. A coin spinning on its edge slows down and just before it comes to rest, makes a noise like "wha-wha-wha-wha-wha." What determines the frequency of this "vibration"? Can you predict the numerical frequency before you test it? Experiment with larger disks and see if they behave in predictable ways.

5. Make a study of how fast birds beat their wings. You

might be able to do this from books on birds, or if you have a video camera you may be able to "film" birds in flight and then find the period of motion of their wings on the screen. Can you make predictions about how fast a bird will flap its wings based on the size of its wings?

6. When armies go across a bridge, they don't march in step. Is there a reason why marching in step might be a problem? Design an experiment to investigate this possibility.

7. Water sloshes back and forth in a pan of water, but how fast does it go? Run some experiments so that you can predict the period of motion for a pan before you actually test it. You can start with a baking pan and then try an aquarium or roasting pan. You should vary the depth of the water as well as the container size. You may be able to try this experiment in a sink or the bathtub. Would a swimming pool be too big?

HOW SOUNDS ARE MADE:
WHY THEY ALL SEEM DIFFERENT

We experience all different kinds of sounds. Sounds have different pitches and different "qualities." The different qualities allow us to tell the difference between a trombone and a guitar playing the same note, but how can we do this? Both vibrate at the same frequency so shouldn't they sound the same? The difference is that they vibrate at other frequencies as well, and the strength of those frequencies determines the quality of the sound.

Quite obviously, everyone has slightly different vocal cords, throat, and mouth, which make their speech "characteristic" of them. But why do people sound different over the phone? Is it that we don't hear all of the frequencies produced by the voice? Why don't you sound the same when you hear a recording of your voice? Why does a live concert sound different than a recorded one?

You can run some simple experiments to see what happens when frequencies are missing and then you can use that knowledge to look more closely at how you hear things. Try to make a hypothesis about the results of your experiments before you actually run them and then see if your hypothesis is correct. Remember, your hypothesis is just a guess and not even Nobel Prize winners guess right all the time.

MATERIALS AND TOOLS
guitar
guitar pick

Place the guitar on a flat surface which will not scratch the back of the guitar. Pluck a string and listen to the pitch. Pluck the other strings and listen to their pitch. What differences do you hear?

Place your finger firmly on a string near one of the frets (the bands which go across the neck) and then pluck the string with the other hand. How does the pitch change?

Now pluck the string with your finger in different places along the string: in the middle, where it is normally plucked, and right next to the bridge (where the string is attached). What differences do you hear? Which positions seem to amplify the higher pitches and sound different?

Play a scale on the low string: do, re, mi . . . do. Notice how this high "do" sounds. Then pluck the string while gently holding your finger on the string over the fret you used to play the high "do." Quickly remove your finger. You will be playing what is known as the second "harmonic." (You may want to ask a person who knows how to play a guitar how to do this if you don't know how.) How does this note sound as compared to the first high "do" you played? Is the pitch the same? Does it *sound* the same?

Compare the sound produced when the friend pushes firmly on the front of the guitar. Does it sound different? Why might this be so?

Think about the physics of the guitar.
Why is the top string lowest in pitch?
How does tightening a string create
a higher pitch?

Use a pick and try to figure out why the quality of the sound changes. Is it like any other sound you produced in the experiment? Why might that be so?

What other sounds can you produce with the guitar? What makes the sounds sound different? The differences in the quality of the pitches are related to the strength of the harmonics which are played. The "tinny" sounds are the ones which emphasize the higher frequencies or higher harmonics. The rich tones tend to emphasize the lower frequencies. What different ways do you play the guitar to produce each of these different sounds?

OTHER PROJECTS WITH SOUND

1. Compare the way different shaped or different types of guitars sound and see if you can figure why they sound different. Cheap guitars generally sound worse than more expensive ones. Can you find out why?

2. Make a study of how various instruments in an orchestra sound and try to relate the quality of their sounds to what they are made from and how they are played.

3. Use a wind instrument to find how the pitch and tone change under different conditions. What happens when a mute or your hand is placed in the open end of the instrument? Why might this change occur? What changes occur as the mute is put farther and farther into the bell of the trumpet?

4. If you can use an oscilloscope from a science lab, attach it to a microphone; then you can look more closely at the different frequencies making up a sound. Different

**An oscilloscope trace
showing a sound wave of
constant frequency**

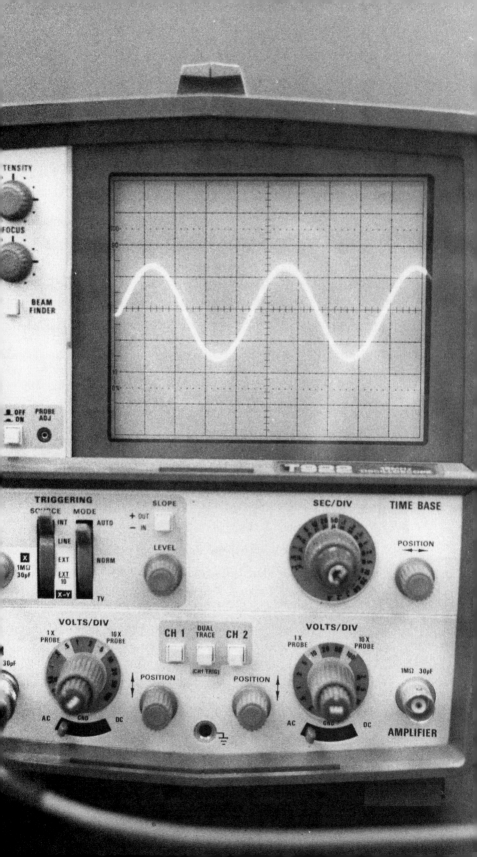

instruments have different patterns of waves. The oscilloscope shows graphically some of the differences you hear in the simple experiment with the guitar. Repeat that experiment and try to relate what you see on the screen to what you hear. See what your voice "looks" like when spoken directly into the microphone as compared to coming over the phone. Try singing a single pitch. Can you get a perfect sine wave?

5. All musical instruments produce harmonics, meaning that they produce more than one frequency. The harmonics are associated with "standing waves" or natural frequencies in the instrument. A wave is very close to a sine wave, but adding two or more waves of different frequencies together makes the wave look complex. This is what you "see" when you look at the waves with an oscilloscope.

Write a computer program to plot a sine wave on the screen. Then modify the program so that you can plot the sum of two (or more) sine waves with different frequencies and amplitudes. This allows you to display harmonics on the screen. Generally, the harmonics are integer multiples of the fundamental frequency so if you make a wave with 1 cycle/sec (the fundamental frequency), then the harmonics would be 2, 3, 4, . . . cycles/sec. This makes writing the program relatively easy.

HOW ELECTRIC CURRENT IS REGULATED: ON, OFF AND MEDIUM

Electricity is a wonderful thing, but generally we want to be able to regulate it. Most lights are turned on and off, refrigerators turn off when the temperature is right, and knobs on a stereo adjust the volume. Only a few things, like electric clocks, are always left on and don't need switches of any kind.

Most appliances use devices which let more or less electricity through them at different times, but how is this done? How can electricity be used to measure temperature, make a telephone ring, or change the volume of a stereo? How do these devices change the amount of current which flows? How does a transistor change the current flowing in a circuit, and how can it "amplify" an electric current?

Many switches take advantage of Ohm's law, which states that the current (in amps) equals the voltage (in volts) divided by the resistance (in ohms). The higher the resistance, the lower the current. Some devices, like the transistor, are different and are called non-ohmic devices.

A few simple experiments with switches can help you to understand how they work and a little more about electrical resistance. These experiments are just the beginning. If you become involved in this kind of thing, you may be working on computer designs or exotic electronic components. Obviously, there is more to electric circuits than is presented here.

In order to study these electrical devices, you need a meter which measures current. If you can borrow one from a science lab, then you can do the rest of the experiments without building a meter. However, building a meter is fun and allows you to see how one works.

Building a Meter
MATERIALS AND TOOLS
thin insulated wire 2 m long
compass
tape
dry cell battery

PROCEDURE
Wind the wire into a coil just large enough to allow you to put the compass inside it. Wrap tape around the coil so it doesn't uncoil and lose its shape. Leave straight ends of the wire about 10 cm long so that you can attach the wire to a battery or other wires.

Place the compass in the loop so the compass is in the horizontal plane. The coil should be pointed north-south. In order to have the coil stay in this position, you may have to build a little cardboard stand for it.

Strip the insulation off the ends of the straight sections of wire so when they touch the poles of the battery they will conduct electricity.

Attach one wire on one end of the battery with tape and then briefly touch the other wire to the other end of the battery. What happens?

Try switching wires on the battery. What happens?

Your meter is not as good as ones used in most science labs, but it will allow you to see changes in current.

The Experiments

MATERIALS AND TOOLS
tape
two 1.5-volt batteries
wire (it should have insulation on it except at the ends)
electric meter to measure current (an ammeter)
regular switch
ten 10-ohm resistors
Note: This kind of electrical equipment can be purchased at stores like Radio Shack.

PROCEDURE

Caution: **In running all of these experiments with batteries, immediately remove the wires from the battery if the battery gets hot.**

Tape a wire which goes to an electric meter to one end of the dry cell. If the meter has a positive and negative side to it, make sure that the positive side is attached to the positive side of the battery. If you borrow a meter, make sure that the meter can measure 1 amp of current. If it measures much more than this, it's hard to see the differences in current, and if it measures much less than 1 amp, you may burn it out unless it has a fuse.

Attach wires so current flows (when you connect the last wire to the battery) from the battery through the meter, through a 10-ohm resistor, through the switch, and back to the battery, as shown in Figure 12. Make sure that the switch is in the "off" or open position so that no current will flow through it when you hook up your circuit.

When you have everything set up correctly, *briefly* close the switch or turn it to the "on" position. **If the meter needle goes past the end of the scale, open the switch immediately or you may burn out your meter. Follow this procedure every time you change the circuit.** If you are using a meter you build using the directions above, you don't have to worry about burning out your meter.

If you had to open your switch because too much current was flowing, add a few more resistors so the current must flow through one after the other, meaning that they are in *series*. Then try again.

What happens to the resistance of the circuit when the switch is closed or opened?

What happens if you add a few more resistors to the circuit? Does the current in your meter change? What happens when you double the resistance of the circuit by adding another resistor in series? What happens when you use two batteries?

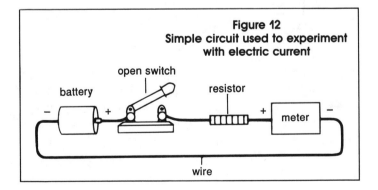

Figure 12
Simple circuit used to experiment with electric current

open switch

battery

resistor

meter

wire

OTHER PROJECTS WITH
ELECTRIC CIRCUITS

1. Use a rheostat (sometimes known as a variable resistor) with a resistance of 10–100 ohms in a circuit. Examine the way it changes the current in your circuit. Be careful not to send too much current through your meter.

2. Get a thermistor with a resistance in the 10-ohm range and see how its resistance changes as the temperature changes. How could you make this into a thermometer?

3. Place a resistor in ice water and find how much current flows. Then place it in boiling water and see what current flows. What differences do you observe? What happens at other temperatures?

4. Find the resistance of various things, using your meter and battery. Make note of the current flowing through the meter with various known resistors. Use this information to find the current through unknown objects. **Make sure when you test some substance that you don't burn out your meter because too much current flows.** Make your connections briefly at first.

5. If you are familiar with how transistors work, find how the resistance of the transistor varies with the "gate" or "base" voltage. Different transistors behave differently so you may want to test different ones.

HOW A GENERATOR WORKS:
CURRENT FROM A WIRE AND A MAGNET

Most of the electricity we use is generated by coils of wire and magnets. In large power-generating plants, magnets are turned near coils of wire. As the magnetic fields change in the coils of wire, current flows to oppose this change in magnetic fields.

But how much current flows in a small coil of wire when a small magnet is brought near it? Under what conditions does it flow? What motions cause current? Which way does the current flow, and can it be controlled?

Lenz's law states that current flows so as to oppose a change in magnetic field in a loop of wire. But what does this mean? It's possible to make a simple generator and run experiments to help answer these questions. You can experiment to see when currents flow and when they don't. You can vary the strength of the magnets, size and number of the loops of wire, etc., and observe the differences.

MATERIALS AND TOOLS
thin wire 3 m long
meter to measure current (homemade or borrowed)
magnet (the stronger the better)
clothes-hanger wire
tape

PROCEDURE
Wrap the middle third of your wire into a loop about 3 cm (1 in) in diameter. This leaves two 1-m-long sections of wire at each end and allows you to experiment a long way from your meter.

Remove the insulation from the ends of the wire and connect them to the meter.

Place the magnet on a table and then bring the coil of wire quickly toward the magnet. Observe your meter for a reaction. What happens? Record your results.

Hold the coil stationary near the magnet. What result do you find?

Move the coil quickly away from the magnet and observe the result. What does your meter do?

(If you have a meter from a science lab, you may find that sometimes the meter wants to go the "wrong way." This means current is flowing in the opposite direction from the way it flows when the meter moves the right way.)

Now, push a short piece of clothes-hanger wire through the coil so you can spin the coil by rolling the wire in your fingers. Tape helps to hold the wire in place.

Bring the coil near the magnet and see if you can make a current flow by spinning the coil between your fingers. What do you observe?

Now tape another piece of clothes-hanger wire to the magnet so you can spin the magnet by rolling the wire in your fingers.

Bring the magnet near the coil of wire which is lying flat on a table and turn the magnet. What happens? Does it matter how fast you turn the magnet? Does it matter how close you have the magnet to the coil?

What other ways can you make current flow in the coil of wire? What seems to be the underlying principle which causes current to flow? Does Lenz's law explain your results?

OTHER PROJECTS WITH GENERATORS

1. Build a windmill or waterwheel which will generate current.

2. Make the device shown in Figure 13 so you can have a coil of wire rotating and still take current from the coil without having the wires get twisted. Make a ring of bare wire on each side of the coil. Then, design a way so that, as the coil spins, a stationary wire will be rubbing against the ring. The stationary wire should always be touching the ring as the ring turns. This makes a "moving" connection or what is called a commutator.

3. Build a spark generator by making current run through a coil of wire with many turns and then quickly removing a wire connected to the power source. Where does the spark appear? Can you think of any way to use this device to build a charcoal-fire starter?

HOW YOU CAN SEE MAGNETIC FIELDS: A FORCE FIELD

Magnetic fields are areas where a force is exerted on a magnet. Their shape is important to scientists because

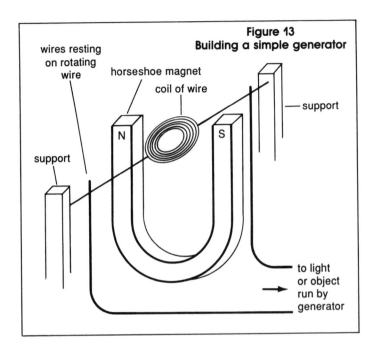

Figure 13
Building a simple generator

wires resting on rotating wire

horseshoe magnet

coil of wire

support

N   S

support

to light or object run by generator

magnetic fields affect how charged particles move. Recently, the Earth's magnetic field has been causing problems because there is a "hole," or weak spot, just off the coast of Brazil. This allows charged particles which normally stay 800 km (500 mi) above the Earth to come to half that distance. Spacecraft are hit by these particles whenever they pass through this hole. The particles cause loss of computer memory, strange data coming from sensors, and many other annoying effects.

But how can you "see" magnetic fields? What is the shape of them, and how do they interact with other magnetic fields? What happens when two magnets are placed near each other? Does the field from an electromagnet look any different from that of a permanent magnet?

Magnetic fields around magnets and coils of wire are interesting to observe. Running a simple experiment can help you to understand the shape of the fields. As you see the fields, try to relate their shape to the shape of the magnet.

MATERIALS AND TOOLS
small compass
sheets of paper
a few magnets of different shapes
pencil
thin wire 2 m long
flashlight battery

PROCEDURE
Place the compass on a table, making sure that all magnets are a long way from the compass. Find which way it points. Record this direction.

Place a piece of paper on the table and a magnet on top of it. Trace the shape of the magnet so later you can see where it was.

Now place the compass near the magnet and observe the direction the needle points to. Indicate that direction by drawing an arrow as in Figure 14.

Move the compass to other positions around the magnet, varying the distance to the magnet as well. Draw arrows indicating the direction the compass needle points.

Now place the compass a long way from the magnet. To which direction does the needle point? Slowly move the compass toward the magnet. What does this mean about the way the compass needle behaves?

Draw a diagram showing the field's shape. Realize that the compass points because of a combination of forces from the magnet and the Earth's magnetic field.

Use a new piece of paper and a magnet of a different shape and repeat the experiment. What differences do you expect in the shape of the field, and do the actual differences agree with what you expected?

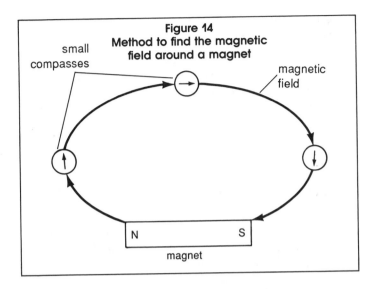

Figure 14
Method to find the magnetic field around a magnet

small compasses

magnetic field

N   S

magnet

Make a coil of wire 3 cm (1 in) in diameter out of thin wire. Put this on the paper so that the coil is in the vertical plane, that is, is standing on edge.

Attach the coil to a battery with tape (you will have to remove the insulation on the ends of the wire). Then draw the field lines around the coil. Attach the wires for as brief a time as possible. **Immediately remove the wires from the battery if it gets hot.**

OTHER PROJECTS WITH MAGNETIC FIELDS

1. Examine the fields made by two or more magnets. Can you predict the shape of the field?

2. Sometimes an area of uniform magnetic field is desired. Can you use two or more magnets to form such a field?

3. Find appliances or toys with magnets in them and see if you can figure out how the magnets must be placed in order to create the fields.

HOW YOU CAN USE ELECTROMAGNETS:
THEY TURN ON AND OFF

Electromagnets are often more useful than permanent magnets because they can be turned off or on. This kind of magnet is used in buzzers, some types of switches, record players, tape decks, VCRs, and hundreds of other devices.

But how can you make a switch that will turn itself on and off? What happens when you make and break the connection going to the coil of wire? How fast does the field change as you turn the current on and off?

Making an electromagnet which can be switched on and off can be an interesting project in itself. But beyond that, you can use your electromagnet to solve a number of problems. As you experiment with electromagnets, you can learn more about how and why they work, as well as how other common household devices work. Electromagnets are made from coils of wire carrying current. Sometimes they have an iron core, which concentrates the field. The number of different kinds of things that use magnets is amazing.

MATERIALS AND TOOLS
5 m (15 ft) of insulated wire, such as speaker wire
piece of copper or aluminum tubing 10 cm (3 in) long
    and 1 cm (1/4 in) in diameter
tape
1.5-volt battery
switch
iron nail which fits into the tube
assorted other iron nails
wooden blocks
strips of steel from a "tin" can

PROCEDURE
Wrap the wire around the tubing, starting at one end. When you get to the other end of the tubing, start back

with a second layer, etc. Leave about 20 cm (6 in) of wire unwrapped so you can connect the coil to a battery.

After you have made your coil, wind a layer of tape on the wire so it doesn't unwind.

Remove 1 cm of insulation from the wires so you can connect them to a battery.

Attach one wire to one terminal of the battery with a piece of tape. The other wire should go to the switch. Connect the other side of the switch to the battery. Make sure the switch is in the open position so no current flows as you make the connections.

Now, put a few nails on a table and close the switch. See how many nails you can pick up with your coil of wire. Don't leave the battery connected too long, for it will go dead very quickly if you do. If the battery starts to get warm, don't use it until it cools.

Now, insert a nail into the tubing, taping it in place. Reconnect the wire and observe any differences.

Using wood blocks, build a setup like the one shown in Figure 15. Attach a strip of steel about 2 cm (.8 in) wide to a block of wood so it sticks out over the edge as shown. Finally, attach your coil to the block. The distance between the coil and the steel strip should be about .5 cm (1/4 in).

What happens as current starts and stops in the coil?

Can you figure how you could make an electric switch that turns something on and off using your coil?

OTHER PROJECTS WITH ELECTROMAGNETS

1. Using an electromagnet, make a switch which can turn a flashlight bulb on and off.

2. Make a buzzer that operates using a coil of wire and a power source. You must design it so that when current goes through the coil, it makes the clapper of the buzzer move toward the coil. However, as the clapper

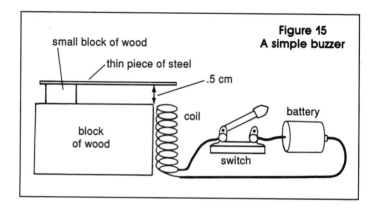

Figure 15
A simple buzzer

small block of wood

thin piece of steel

.5 cm

coil

battery

block
of wood

switch

moves toward the coil, it must disconnect the power source, which means the clapper isn't attracted to the coil. The clapper moves away, the connection is made again, current flows, and the process repeats.

3. Investigate what things affect the frequency at which an electric buzzer rings.

4. Design and build an electric lock which can lock a door. How should you design it so that you can open it if the battery goes dead?

5. Sprinkle iron filings on a sheet of paper and then slowly move the coil of wire across the paper as you turn the current on and off. What happens to the filings? This is similar to what happens to the magnetic particles in magnetic tapes used in tape recorders and VCRs. What happens when you change the speed of motion or the strength of the magnet?

OTHER PROJECTS WITH WAVES, ELECTRICITY, AND MAGNETISM

1. Examine the conditions which cause you to get shocks as you walk across a carpet.

2. How can you make a current flow with just a magnet and a rotating metal disk? This is how Edison made current for his light bulbs.

3. Experiment with solar cells. See how much current and how much voltage they produce.

4. Get a low-voltage power supply from a science department and then examine how much heating you get from different resistors attached in different ways. What affects the power lost as heat?

5. Investigate how transistors can be used to amplify current. There are many books on how to make circuits, and these can help you get started with your experiments.

6. Run experiments to see how the resistance of a light bulb changes with its temperature. Do all light bulbs change in the same way?

7. Make a windmill that generates electricity. Devise the best generator for the speed at which the windmill blades will turn.

8. Learn how to read the electric meter in your house and see how your electric usage varies from week to week, season to season.

FOR FURTHER READING

Berg, Richard. *Physics of Sound.* Englewood Cliffs, N.J.: Prentice-Hall, 1982.

Hunter, Ilene, and Marilyn Judson. *Simple Folk Instruments to Make and Play.* New York: Simon and Schuster, 1977.

Pierce, John. *The Science of Musical Sound.* New York: W. H. Freeman, 1983.

Scott, John. *Electricity, Electronics and You.* Portland, Maine: J. Weston Walch, 1981.

APPENDIX

SCIENCE FAIRS

Entering a science project in a science fair can be very rewarding. Sometimes it's just nice to have a goal to work toward, but making a presentation also makes you focus on what you have done. You are forced to look critically at your project and to ask questions about your data and conclusions. Having someone point out a flaw in your reasoning which you can't defend can be embarrassing. Make sure that you have analyzed the data thoroughly or you may be disappointed.

Your project is judged on the basis of originality, presentation, and scientific content. Other people may have done projects similar to yours in the past, but yours should have a new viewpoint or method to collect data. You must also show that you understand what you did and show that your conclusions are based on sound principles and good data. You must express your ideas so others can understand what you did and how you reached the conclusions.

Your project will be viewed by many people, and you have to make sure that it answers the questions viewers may ask about your project. You must clearly state what you did, show your data in a logical manner, and indicate how you reached your conclusions. Sometimes preparing for a science fair seems like a lot of work but in the end it helps you to learn more from your project.

PRESENTATION

Your project will be viewed by others who will want to understand what you have done, so you must think about how to present it clearly and concisely. It should also catch the eye of people who walk past. First impressions do make a difference: if your project doesn't initially catch the attention of viewers, they may not stop to learn about it. Make your project look good, but don't sacrifice science in the process.

Before you start working on the presentation, review your experiment from beginning to end:

1. Think of the original hypothesis and design of your project.

2. Review notes you may have taken on any reading you did related to your project.

3. Look over your data and observations, noting anything which might seem strange or inconsistent.

4. See if your graphs and tables make sense.

5. Make sure that your conclusions follow from your data and that you can't interpret the data in some other way.

Once you have thought about the five things mentioned above, it's time to start writing. It's not always easy to write the report, but it's a necessary step in presenting your findings. And if scientists did not present their discoveries, other scientists might have to discover them again. Generally, once you get started writing, things get easier. Some people may find making the presentation is as hard as doing the project. For others, it will be easier.

Your report should be formal, with a title page giving the name of your project, your name, school, address, and the date. The exact way the title page should be written may vary from one science fair to another. You should also give credit to and thank the people who helped you or lent you equipment. These people might even want a copy of the paper and to see your project.

You may then have to give a table of contents followed by a statement of purpose (a sentence or two about what you were trying to show). An abstract may follow and is designed to allow readers to quickly find out what you did and what you conclude. This allows them to look at the project more closely if they wish. A sample abstract follows:

MOTION ON ROTATING PLATFORMS
Mary G. Round
101 Amusement Park Rd.
Carousel, CA

A study was done on a rotating platform to see the path of a rolling ball relative to the platform. Because the ball rolls, the path will not be the same as if it were just sliding across a smooth surface. Hollow and solid balls of different sizes were used. It was shown that the path taken by the balls was similar to the one predicted by a computer model.

The background section of the report contains the information you found from books and the scientific principles you used to analyze your data. You should briefly discuss what you have read and why it is important.

The section discussing how you ran the experiment

should include a description of the apparatus, generally with photographs and drawings if you can't present the actual apparatus. A person reading your report should be able to tell exactly what you did and why you did it. Make sure that things are clearly labeled.

Your data and conclusions should be presented in a logical and clear form. Graphs and tables may help to present the ideas clearly. If the data is not clearly presented, a person trying to understand it may miss important information and reach improper conclusions, ones different from yours. You should also mention how precise you think your results are. Be realistic, so you won't have someone ask you an embarrassing question.

The bibliography finishes the report and is a list of books, articles, and other sources you used for your paper. These should be listed in alphabetical order by author (with the last name first). You should also include the page number if you used specific information rather than just general information from the whole book or article.

INDEX

ABOUT THE
AUTHOR

Peter Goodwin teaches high school physics and astronomy and also chairs the science department at the Kent School in Kent, Connecticut. He holds a B.A. in physics from Middlebury College and an M.A. in education from Trinity College. Mr. Goodwin has also written *Engineering Projects for Young Scientists* for Franklin Watts. His hobbies include photography, playing the guitar, canoeing, cross-country skiing, orienteering, and gardening in his solar greenhouse. He lives with his wife, Susan, and two sons in a house he built himself.